Praise for *The Emigrant Edge*

"Brian's thoughtful, compelling, and practical book helps you reap the advantages of a positive brain by transforming gratitude and optimism into fuel for success."

—Shawn Achor, happiness researcher and *New York Times* bestselling author of *The Happiness Advantage and Before Happiness*

"We all know people who weren't born here but have become hugely successful. Brian Buffini not only personifies the spirit of these people, he's found the common threads of why so many newcomers make it big in America. And in this book he reveals them for the first time ever."

—Dave Liniger, CEO, chairman of the board and cofounder of RE/MAX, LLC

"In *The Emigrant Edge*, Brian Buffini has revealed the seven character traits of how to succeed in America."

—Jack Canfield, coauthor of the #1 *New York Times* bestselling Chicken Soup for the Soul® series and *The Success Principles*™

"Dad called it the 'GOSH!' attitude. Brian Buffini calls it the Emigrant Edge. What is it? The ability to see that in America we are surrounded by opportunity—if only we will just look for it. Are you ready to see the opportunities that surround you? Fantastic! Start reading *The Emigrant Edge* right now!"

—Tom Ziglar, CEO, Ziglar, Inc.

"I love Brian Buffini and his awe-inspiring immigrant rags-to-riches story. In *The Emigrant Edge*, he reveals how he did it and how you, too, can make it big in America!"

—Darren Hardy, founding publisher/editor *SUCCESS* magazine, *New York Times* bestselling author, and CEO mentor

"There is nothing more powerful than making a way out of no way, beating the odds, and snatching victory from the jaws of defeat. Brian Buffini's *The Emigrant Edge* offers principles for every person fighting to get unstuck and find their life's purpose. After reading this book, your mind will expand, and you will be uncomfortable until you fulfill your life's calling no matter what the circumstances."

—Les Brown, bestselling author and speaker

"Brian Buffini is one of the world's leading experts on peak performance and people development. In this book, he persuasively chronicles proven fundamentals and beliefs that enable immigrants to excel in the land of the free and the home of the brave."

—Dr. Nido R. Qubein, president, High Point University

"Brian Buffini's *The Emigrant Edge* will remind you that America is ripe with opportunity and that dreams can come true. And not only that, he outlines the 'success formula' that he and other immigrants have used to achieve their fortunes. A must read!"

—Brian P. Moran, *New York Times* bestselling author of *The 12 Week Year*

"This is a book of beauty that inspires us all to achieve a fulfilled and happy life. When I began reading, I knew I was reading something special, and I could not put it down because it made so much sense. I learned how expressing gratitude can be a critical component of financial success, and I learned how to incorporate Brian's teachings into my life to make a more powerful positive impact on others. Brian Buffini brilliantly cuts through the obstacles and myths holding you back from reaching your dream. You must read this book!"

—Joel Fuhrman, MD, *New York Times* bestselling author and president, Nutritional Research Foundation

"Brian Buffini is one of my favorite people on the planet—and one of the great influencers of our time. In *The Emigrant Edge*, he shares with us how he has achieved his remarkable success and why so many newcomers make it big in this country. The American Dream is very real, and Brian shows you how to achieve it!"

—Jon Gordon, bestselling author of *The Energy Bus* and *The Carpenter*

"Few people know the traits required for overcoming adversity and achieving true success better than Brian Buffini. In *The Emigrant Edge*, Brian shares his amazing life story of growing up in Ireland, journeying to the United States, the struggles faced, the lessons learned, and, ultimately, the success attained. This man is a diligent student of success, is friends with some of the most profoundly important leadership gurus of our time, and uses his life experiences to encourage others to achieve success, too."

—John O'Leary, #1 national bestselling author of *On Fire*

"Gratitude is a superpower. It is a source of empathy, authenticity, joy, and connectedness to ourselves and others. In *The Emigrant Edge*, Brian Buffini outlines practical examples by which to leverage our hard work and gratitude as a competitive advantage in business. Brian has been a mentor of mine for the last five years and has helped me shape my brand, my business, and my own ability to endure hardship and express my sincere gratefulness for life. So it is with deep heartfelt sincerity that I proudly endorse this book. Enjoy."

—Erik Wahl, graffiti artist and bestselling author of *Unthink*

"Brian Buffini is the living embodiment of the American Dream— incredibly successful in his own business, a man on a mission to inspire others, and a husband and a father to six amazing kids. His celebration of immigrants like himself who make this country what it is as its best couldn't come at a better time. The best testimonial I can give is that fifteen years ago Brian inspired me to believe I could build my own new business and helped me to do it for no other reason than he believed in me. This book is a step-by-step distillation of his method, and I felt inspired all over again."

—Tony Schwartz, CEO, The Energy Project, and bestselling author of *The Power of Full Engagement* and *The Way We're Working Isn't Working*

"This emigrant from Ireland with an Italian last name and an Irish brogue has become the preeminent coach throughout corporate America. Brian's eminently readable work serves as a wake-up call and plan for all those merely dreaming the American Dream."

—Gino Blefari, CEO, HSF Affiliates LLC

"More than 250 years ago, my ancestors traveled from Europe to what would become America. I know that they would be proud of what their descendants have accomplished. The courage, commitment, and work ethic that it takes to build a new life in a foreign land remain much the same today. I want people with these qualities on my team. These are the qualities that Brian has studied, pondered, and presented on these pages for all to learn, live by, and prosper."

—Phil Soper, president and CEO, Royal LePage

"What is it that enables immigrants to come to America and live the American Dream when so many US citizens can't seem to achieve what they want in life? These immigrants thrive no matter the barriers that stand in their way, while many people born in America can't seem to get past everyday roadblocks. In *The Emigrant Edge*, Brian Buffini shares seven strategies to show you how to think like an emigrant in order to develop a winning mind-set. You, too, will be able to use your head to bust through barriers and emerge even stronger . . . without so much as a concussion."

—Alison Levine, author of the *New York Times* bestseller *On the Edge: Leadership Lessons from Everest and Other Extreme Environments*

"Packed with fascinating anecdotes and enduring lessons from Brian's life, *The Emigrant Edge* calls us to claim our predecessors' strengths as our own. At a time of dystopian divisiveness, we need more efforts like Brian's to bridge the gaps with, and admire the contributions of, people with differing backgrounds."

—Aron Ralston, public speaker, adventurer, and subject of the movie *127 Hours*

"Brian has nailed it. Doing business with an open heart, an open mind, and a willingness to do what it takes, he shows that you can succeed—not in spite of where you've come from, but because of it. It will truly give you the Edge."

—Scott Stratten, president, UnMarketing Inc.

"Brian Buffini's rags-to-riches story of success is the ultimate master class in making it in America."

—Dr. Ivan Misner, founder of BNI and *New York Times* bestselling author

"In *The Emigrant Edge*, Brian Buffini shows us the secrets of making it big in America."

—Dan Buettner, National Geographic fellow and *New York Times* bestselling author of *The Blue Zones*

The
EMIGRANT
EDGE

How to Make It Big in America

BRIAN BUFFINI

HOWARD BOOKS
AN IMPRINT OF SIMON & SCHUSTER, INC.

New York   London   Toronto   Sydney   New Delhi

Howard Books
An Imprint of Simon & Schuster, Inc.
1230 Avenue of the Americas
New York, NY 10020

First Howard Books hardcover edition August 2017

HOWARD and colophon are trademarks of Simon & Schuster, Inc.

For information about special discounts for bulk purchases,
please contact Simon & Schuster Special Sales at 1-866-506-1949
or business@simonandschuster.com.

The Simon & Schuster Speakers Bureau can bring authors to your live event. For more information or to book an event, contact the Simon & Schuster Speakers Bureau at 1-866-248-3049 or visit our website at www.simonspeakers.com.

Interior design by Davina Mock-Maniscalco

Manufactured in the United States of America

10 9 8 7 6 5 4 3 2

Library of Congress Cataloging-in-Publication Data is available.

ISBN 978-1-5011-6927-4
ISBN 978-1-5011-6929-8 (ebook)

To every courageous person
who ever packed everything they owned into a suitcase
and left everyone they loved to pursue their dream.
You are the fabric of every great society.

CONTENTS

CONTENTS

CONTENTS

CONTENTS

Preface

How You Can Attain the Emigrant Edge

know what you're thinking: *I've just picked up a book written by a guy who can't even spell!* That word in the title should read immigrant, not emigrant, right? Let me explain. An emigrant is a person who leaves his or her own country to permanently settle in another. When you leave your homeland you're an emigrant, but when you arrive at your new destination you're an immigrant.

I'm Irish, and where I come from emigration is a very big deal. For the past 150 years, Ireland's greatest export has been its people. Many families in Ireland have lost a son or daughter to emigration—my own parents saw all five of their sons move to America.

I moved to this great country as a nineteen-year-old with ninety-two dollars in my pocket, and now I'm a wealthy businessman. I'm the classic American rags-to-riches story. But I haven't just acquired material wealth since I came here. I also possess a priceless internal fulfillment that no amount of money could buy.

Why have I succeeded when people who are born and raised here haven't? I believe I have the Emigrant Edge—a special mix of qualities and traits that have given me a head start over native-born Americans. My promise to you is that no matter where you're from, you too can adopt these traits in your own life and attain success beyond your wildest dreams. And I can show you how.

Now, I'm not saying that making it big in America is simple. It's not simple—there are definite things you'll need to add to your life if you want great success. But the seven strategies I share in this book are easy. They're easy to grasp and, in all truth, easy to implement. It just takes a committed mind-set and consistent follow-through.

My life's work has been dedicated to teaching and training people how to live the American Dream. Now, the American Dream means different things to different people, but let's consider a classic definition for a moment. In his 1931 book, *The Epic of America,* historian James Truslow Adams defined the American Dream as "a land in which life should be better and richer and fuller for every man, with opportunity for each according to his ability or achievement."

In my experience, this explanation encapsulates what the American Dream is all about. For the past twenty years, I've presented my success strategies to three million people at seminars and events all over the world, and I've had a lot of opportunities to listen to people's thoughts, feelings, and beliefs about this topic. American audiences have always been the most enthusiastic and ambitious about their future. However, in recent years, things have changed. I've begun to notice a shift. I've found myself working harder and harder to convince people that a better future lies ahead, that their children can have more opportunities than they did growing up, and that the sky is still the limit when it comes to achieving success in America. I've been spending a lot of my time reminding Americans who they are, what they've accomplished as a nation, and how great their future can be!

This shift in thinking and attitude isn't just cosmetic or superficial—it's profound. Many Americans I encounter now believe that the ideal of the American Dream is out of reach, or doesn't even exist. In fact, according to a recent survey from Harvard's Institute of Politics, more than 50 percent of Millennials no longer think the American Dream is possible at all. My advice to those folks? Go travel the world and get some perspective. Seeing how much less people in other countries have compared with us will open your eyes to how good we have it here! Take it from me, when you arrive back home you'll kiss the ground. The American Dream *is* still alive, and it's not nearly as difficult to achieve as you might expect.

A fish discovers water last. In other words, you can be surrounded by everything you need to succeed but still be oblivious to it. That's exactly how it is for many Americans today. Every year, millions of people battle to move to this great country, but many of those who were actually born and raised here seem to think they have life hard. I sometimes think that the only people who don't know how great America is are Americans!

Now, I'm not saying that people don't experience genuine hardship in this country, because they do. But, for most, life is far easier here than it is for people living under repressive regimes around the globe. In his book *The Haves and the Have-Nots,* World Bank economist Branko Milanović outlined how even the poorest among us are richer than most of the world. The fact is that the majority of us have little to complain about when it comes to the ease of our everyday living, but we still manage to find fault with plenty. We grumble when the Wi-Fi doesn't connect, we moan when our caramel macchiato is too frothy, and we whine if our fast food is too slow. I've been to places where they don't have much fast *or* slow food. People in other corners of the globe would love to have the issues we fuss over. So why is it that, even though we're surrounded by plenty and have so much to be grateful for, we get hung up on trivial irritations? It's because we've lost perspective! We've lived with such an overabundance for so long that we've forgotten how hard generations before us had to work to afford us the conveniences we have today. What was once considered the good fortune of a lifetime, we now see as an everyday occurrence. We've forgotten that, in spite of any challenges we might face, we're fortunate to have the inalienable rights to life, liberty, and the pursuit of happiness that are still denied to many in lesser-developed countries.

There are those, however, who haven't forgotten. They continually see this country with fresh eyes. They recognize the opportunities, benefits, and values that our society as a whole offers—and they're ready to work hard and take advantage of them. Who are these people? Immigrants.

To me, and many other immigrants just like me, America is the land where dreams can come true if you apply yourself. This is the mind-set of a successful immigrant—and it's a winning one. Immigrants can teach us a lot about success. People have come from all over the world to settle here and millions of them have thrived. Why do they do well when so many people who are born and raised here fail? Like me, they have the Emigrant Edge!

Successful immigrants think and work differently than the average American. They have a survivor mentality. Many of them have already risked everything they have to start a new life, so a few setbacks on the road to starting and growing a business aren't going to stop them. They are pragmatic rather than idealistic about what it takes to succeed. They know all too well that the world doesn't owe them a living and that each individual is responsible for his or her success. They manage to do a lot with very little, not only because they're resourceful self-starters, but because they don't have a safety net if they fall. Above all, they're willing to pay the price required to succeed. This relentless work ethic, drive, and can-do attitude means they're prepared to start from scratch, work the hours needed, and invest in themselves and their business. They don't see this as a disadvantage, but as a fact—a reality. They can adapt to whatever life throws at them because they're realistic about the challenges they know will come, and they're prepared for overcoming them. They duck and dive and go with the flow or create a new way to overcome if necessary—whatever it takes to defeat the odds—because they're clear about what they want, they're willing to work hard for it, and they never give up. If only every business owner could tap into this mind-set, maybe we could reverse the current trend where approximately 50 percent of small businesses fail within the first five years.

I'm not, for a minute, saying that all immigrants are successful. However, I have become a student of success, and I've seen a consistent pattern among America's most successful immigrants. I've broken down what they do, and I've also analyzed my own journey.

All successful immigrants share seven main characteristics or traits. These are the differentiators between success and failure, winning and losing, a life of prosperity and one of quiet despair. The good news is these seven traits—the Emigrant Edge—are 100 percent transferable and adaptable, no matter where a person is born or what his or her circumstances are. If you imitate these seven traits, you can tap into the DNA of who you are: You'll be better able to access the Emigrant Edge spirit in your own heart, mind, and bloodline so you can attain the same level of achievement that so many newcomers to this country experience.

The truth is, many people living here have no idea how hard it is to succeed in other countries where entrepreneurship, free markets, freedom of speech, and freedom of religion and expression are not even permitted. Life, liberty, and the pursuit of happiness are still promised in America. So while it's not simple to succeed here, it is easier than in many other places you could go. You just need to harness the Emigrant Edge in your life—and I'm going to show you how.

To have an Emigrant Edge, you don't have to move far away from home—you don't even have to move up the street. You just have to learn by example—study the traits of those who have this edge—and then move outside of your comfortable, old way of doing things and apply these traits to your own life. Think and behave like a newcomer and you'll be able to achieve whatever you desire. If you can rediscover and reconnect with the mind-set of previous generations, you will experience phenomenal success, just as many millions have before you.

Are you ready to gain the edge?

Brian Buffini
Founder, Buffini & Company

The
EMIGRANT
EDGE

STRANGER IN A STRANGE LAND

The Natural Disadvantages of Immigrants

Introduction to Part One

Everywhere immigrants have enriched and
strengthened the fabric of American life.

—JOHN F. KENNEDY

More than two hundred years have passed since America's Founding Fathers declared their independence on July 4, 1776. On this date they claimed freedom, not only for themselves and their countrymen but also for millions of immigrants who would come to this country in the future. The founders steadfastly believed that immigration would be the key to the success of their fledgling nation. Unlike King George III of Great Britain, who had barred new European migration because he believed the colonies were becoming too populated and independent, our founders were determined to permit and encourage the influx of people to strengthen the economy. Thomas Jefferson, Benjamin Franklin, and John Adams felt so strongly about it, they detailed a "train of abuses" against the king and demanded an overthrow of the oppressive monarch. They stated that the king had "endeavored to prevent the population of these States; for that purpose obstructing the Laws for Naturalization of Foreigners; refusing to pass others to encourage their migrations hither, and raising the conditions of new Appropriations of Lands."

The American landscape has certainly changed since that first Fourth of July. According to the Migration Policy Institute, in 2014 the American immigrant population stood at more than 42.4 million, or 13.3 percent of the total population of 318.9 million.* Between 2013 and 2014 alone, the foreign-born population increased by 1 million, or 2.5 percent.

Numerical Size and Share of the Foreign-Born Population in the United States, 1970–2014

Year	Size of Immigrant Population (Millions)	Immigrant Share of Total U.S. Population (%)
1970	9.6	4.7
1980	14.1	6.2
1990	19.8	7.9
2000	31.1	11.1
2010	40.0	12.9
2014	42.4	13.3

Migration Policy Institute (MPI) tabulation of data from the U.S. Census Bureau's 2010 and 2014 American Community Surveys (ACS), and 1970–2000 Decennial Census.

Today, according to the Migration Policy Institute, immigrants in the United States and their American-born children number approximately 81 million, or 26 percent of the overall population. Those who have become extremely successful, wealthy people had to over-

---

* The U.S. Census Bureau's 2014 American Community Survey data.

come a series of disadvantages to get to where they are today. However, it's fair to say they have also had certain advantages that have helped them achieve this incredible success. What are these advantages and disadvantages and what can they teach us? Read on and you'll find out.

CHAPTER ONE

Disadvantage One:

Immigrants Don't Understand
Their New Culture

When you leave your home country and move to a different one, you become a stranger in a strange land. Nothing is familiar, nothing feels comfortable, and the simplest of tasks can present difficulties. Whether you encounter barriers from the differences in culture, language, or customs, you face challenges that can make you feel like a vulnerable child. From ordering a sandwich to figuring out how to work the shower faucet handles, being a newcomer comes with an inherent series of disadvantages. As you read and learn about these challenges, you'll realize that an immigrant's *disadvantage* is your *advantage*. You'll discover how, if this were a race, you'd already be many steps ahead.

Most of us have heard the expression, "When in Rome, do as the Romans do." This means that to more easily adapt to the customs and traditions of your new country, you should copy what the natives are doing. But what if you don't understand these customs and traditions or what they mean? Where and how do you even begin to try to fit in?

Coping with culture shock is one of the biggest challenges that immigrants face, and there are many complicated layers to the issue. Newcomers to this country may feel helpless, frustrated, afraid, and insecure about what to do and how to behave. As they continually try to fit in with their new society, they can feel as though they're losing their own cultural identity, beliefs, and values.

A FISH OUT OF WATER

No matter an immigrant's circumstances, from the moment you arrive in this country you're thrown into the deep end. Almost everything is confusing and disconcerting, and being in a strange new environment makes you unsure and uncomfortable everywhere you go. You may not speak the local language, and even if you do, you're still subject to new cultural nuances that make it apparent to everyone that you're an outsider. You might have been the biggest fish in the small pond of your home country, but now you're a small fish in a very large sea. To make matters worse, the waters are far from calm—instead, they can be treacherous with dangerous currents and riptides, making it impossible to feel settled and at ease. Being in this sort of unsteady environment can make you feel like you're drowning when all you want to do is swim with the flow. It can be hard to simply keep your head above water and stay afloat. Just as salmon have to battle to swim upstream to spawn—and only the strongest and the fittest survive—successful immigrants have to battle to find their way in this new world.

WHICH WAY IS UP?

When you're in a new world and trying to adjust to new surroundings, a sense of spatial disorientation can occur. In aviation, spatial disorientation means that a pilot can't correctly interpret the airplane's attitude, altitude, or airspeed in relation to the ground or another point of reference, such as the horizon. When you no longer know where the horizon is, because of poor weather conditions and/or reduced visibility, it can seem like you're flying straight and going in the right direction, but unbeknownst to you, you can actually be plummeting to the ground.

Some immigrants experience this sense of disorientation because they no longer have their own point of reference—their home place—in sight. Their metaphorical horizon has disappeared from view because the language, customs, and culture of their new country are so alien. Even the sounds and smells are different. In their new circumstances, immigrants can feel as though they've been blindfolded and spun in a circle. When they come to a stop, they're dizzy, perplexed, and don't know where true North is. The decisions and choices they make are influenced by this spatial disorientation.

A CHANGE OF PACE

Moving to a new country means a different pace of life, often a faster one. The pace can increase simply as you try to keep up with all the newness and changing circumstances. It can be an overwhelming and exhausting experience, and you can quickly find yourself running on empty. At other times, the pace will slow down, especially if you're in a lull searching for job openings. During those times, it's not unusual to feel isolated without your normal support systems in place. In either case, the change of pace requires adjustment, and those who don't adjust well to change—those who maintain what's called "homeostasis"—inevitably fail.

The term *homeostasis* comes from two Greek words: *homeo*, meaning "similar," and *stasis*, meaning "stable." Homeostasis is the ability of an organism to maintain internal stability when faced with environmental changes, and it's constantly at play in our bodies. You can eat, drink, exercise, and sweat, but your internal body composition—your temperature—always remains at an average of 98.6 degrees. Likewise, if you had blood drawn on ten different days in one month, the levels of sodium, glucose, red blood cells, and other blood components would pretty much stay constant, regardless of what you had been doing. No matter how much water you drink, your body doesn't swell up like a balloon. Similarly, no matter how little you drink, your body doesn't shrivel up like a raisin. The human body knows exactly how much fluid is required and then maintains that constant level. Now, of course, this sort of constancy is a great thing for our bodies, but it's not so great if you want to progress and succeed in a new environment. Immigrants who are unsuccessful inevitably give in to homeostasis and the urge to re-create in the new world exactly what they had in the old one. They stick with the same routines and patterns instead of adapting and finding new ones. Those who succeed take what they've already learned, improve on their knowledge by learning more, and then apply it to their new circumstances.

BRIAN'S STORY

Waterskiing in My Snickers

When I came to America I spoke the language, but almost everything else was completely foreign to me. Most cultural references were in-jokes I didn't understand . . . they all went right over my head. I remember one day a really cute girl asked me to go waterskiing with a group of her friends. Now, I had never been waterskiing in my life. In fact, I couldn't even swim! There was one swimming pool in the part of Dublin I lived in, and some of the lads in the neighborhood used it as a bathtub, if you understand what I mean! So we didn't go to the swimming pool and, take it from me, the Irish Sea is too cold even to dip your toe in. But, being new to California, I was keen to fit in, socialize, and meet new people (and of course I wanted to impress this girl), so I said yes to the invite. After all, one of my main goals when I arrived in this great country was to get a suntan and meet a suntanned girl!

Everyone was really excited about the trip.

"It'll be awesome, totally rad," they all said. I had no idea what "rad" meant, but I went along with it, even though I was convinced I was going to drown. I was going to meet my Maker, I just knew it. On the boat, one of the guys said, "Hey, man, you want a Snickers?" I was thinking, *Snickers? What's a Snickers?* because the only similar word back in Ireland was a slang word for underwear—*knickers*. Here I was about to die waterskiing, and I didn't even have the right underwear on!

So I hit the water, got up for a millisecond, and then did a spectacular face-plant. To add insult to injury, I then forgot to let go of the rope. I was hanging on for dear life because I didn't have the right "Snickers" on, and I was terrified I was going to lose some equipment. I was okay with drowning, but I was not okay with losing my equipment!

After my new friends dragged me out of the water and pumped a gallon or so out of me, the same guy handed me a candy bar and said, "Dude, eat a Snickers." That was when I finally got it—Snickers was chocolate!

I'd love to tell you that this was the only time I literally had no idea what people were saying to me, but in fact that waterskiing incident was only the tip of the iceberg. There were some days I was so lost culturally that it felt like my head was spinning. And guess what? It kept happening for years!

I had already been a real estate agent for quite a while, when one day I got the chance to show a prospective client a $4 million luxury home. It was the first time I had a potential sale for so much money and I was pretty nervous about it. I really wanted to take the buyer on a journey so he could visualize himself in this house. We walked through together, me giving my very best flowery descriptions of the place to inspire this guy. It was going really well—so well, in fact, that I was already spending the commission check in my head!

We got to the patio door and I waved at the magnificent expanse of trees in the garden.

"This place is so special, it even has its own guacamole trees," I pronounced confidently.

The man looked at me strangely. It was only much later I learned that guacamole trees are, of course, avocado trees. Losing a $4 million sale is what it took for me to learn the word *avocado*! That is the essence of a stranger in a strange land!

When you're an immigrant, these kinds of misunderstandings can happen several times a day. But I've learned you can't let them stop you. You have to be willing to try anything and not give up. You have to be brave enough to go waterskiing without your Snickers on! Why? Because you have no other options. And the key to staying determined, even when you *do* get lots of options, is to continue to act as though you don't have any.

I've tried to maintain and stay true to this mindset. If I've established a goal or something I want to achieve, I still try to act as if I have no options, just like I did when I first got here. Because sometimes, by not having any other options, you can clearly see and focus your energy on which direction to take and what move to make next.

CHAPTER TWO

Disadvantage Two:

Immigrants Don't Have Established Relationships

FAMILY MATTERS

One of the hardest things about leaving home is leaving your family behind. For most of us, family provides love, comfort, support, encouragement, companionship, protection, structure, and a framework of values by which we live our lives. Family forms the backbone of who we are—blood really is thicker than water.

Imagine, then, how it feels to leave home and know that you may not get to see your parents or siblings for many years. Immigrants miss birthdays, anniversaries, and holidays with the relatives they leave behind. And it's not just the special occasions that can be lonely. Sometimes it's the casual, everyday interactions with their families that they long for most of all. Dropping by just to say hi for no special reason is something so simple yet so important. Without the emotional support that a family provides, you can feel lost, unsafe, and unstable. It's very easy for a person's mental health to be affected. Studies have discovered that newcomers to America suffer from high rates of depression and "acculturative stress." For example, a 2011 study published in the *Archives of General Psychiatry* found that Mexican immigrants in the United States had rates of depression and anxiety 40 percent higher than nonmigrant relatives remaining in Mexico.

According to Susan J. Matt, a professor of history at Weber State University and the author of *Homesickness: An American History*, immigration may result in opportunity and profits, but it also has high psychological costs. In nearly a decade's worth of research into the emotions and experiences of immigrants, she found that many people who leave home in search of better prospects end up feeling displaced and depressed. However, because it's assumed that individuals can and should be at home anywhere in the world these days, very few are comfortable speaking openly about the pain they experience.

In the past, it was acceptable to admit that migrating was emotionally taxing—medical journals even documented and studied the condition, referring to it by its clinical name: *nostalgia*. Stories of the devastating effects of homesickness used to be common. In 1887, for example, an article in the *Daily Evening Bulletin* of San Francisco had the headline, "Victim of Nostalgia: A Priest Dies Craving for a Sight of His Motherland." It was reported that the Rev. J. M. McHale, a native of Ireland, had fallen ill with nostalgia after arriving in Brooklyn. Shortly before he died, he declared: "I am homesick. My dear country, I will never set a foot on your green shores again. Oh, my mother, how I long to see you."

These days, however, feeling homesick is considered embarrassing, even weak. After all, we have so much technology to keep us in touch with people no matter where they are, so shouldn't moving to a new country be a cinch? We're only one click or phone call away from family, right? Well, yes, Skype is great, but the truth is it can't replace a hug or a personal visit. Actually, sometimes being able to keep such close tabs on family via Facebook, Instagram, or Twitter can make things worse, because you're all too aware of what is happening without you actually being there. There's even a twenty-first-century acronym for this emotion: FOMO—fear of missing out! If you're constantly being reminded of what you're missing, it can be even more difficult to feel at peace and settled, adding to the stress. Believe me, as an immigrant, the emotional ties to the country of your birth are never severed. Even when you succeed and achieve all that you have dreamed of in your new home place, there is always an ache in your heart—and a void in your life—that never goes away.

BIRDS OF A FEATHER—THE UNITY OF COMMUNITY

When you arrive in a new country, you can feel doubly isolated. Besides missing the security and familiarity of family, you also lack the wider blanket of community support and involvement, which adds to your sense of not belonging. This hits hardest those for whom neighborhood and community have traditionally formed a huge part of their lives.

We're all more than the sum of our parts, and a feeling of belonging is a crucial part of our identity. No one wants to go through life alone—we were created to be relational. We need other people to lean on, interact with, and share a common purpose with. However, as a newcomer, the reality is you're on your own. You might know one or two people, but usually that's it. It can be very lonely.

Integrating and becoming a true part of a community can take years. People need to get to know you and accept you. The process is like going to a new school. It takes time and energy to make new friends, form new bonds through shared experiences, and develop lasting relationships that go beyond the school year—and this doesn't happen overnight. You need time to make allies and become a part of groups. But, when you're an immigrant, the time it takes can seem like an eternity.

THE NETWORK IS DOWN

You have no family. You have no community. Now, add to this sense of isolation the fact that you have no professional community to help you get established in a vocation. Oftentimes, in these circumstances, getting a break comes not because of what you know or what you can do, but because of *who* you know and what they can do to help you get to where you want to be. I'm not saying that relying on who you know should ever outweigh a "hard work" mentality, but some doors just can't be opened unless a relationship exists or an introduction is made. If you're new to a country, you haven't had the opportunity to build these networks, associations, or connections yet. You may have the name of a friend of a friend who might know of a job, but unless you happen to be in the right place at the right time, there's no network of people opening doors for you. There's no network of people for you, period. You have to go it alone, no matter what situation you find yourself in.

BRIAN'S STORY

The Motorcycle Accident

I was in America three months when I had a serious motorcycle accident. The situation I found myself in was a waking nightmare. I was badly injured, I had no medical insurance, and I didn't want to call home and tell my parents back in Ireland what had happened, as I knew they'd worry, or, worse, sell their car to fly out and sit by my hospital bed. The only person in all of America I could call was my brother John, who lived one hundred miles away at the time.

John was a little freaked out to hear that I had almost been killed, and he rushed to my bedside as fast as he could. When he arrived, he had a bag with him. What was inside that bag? Clothes? Pajamas? Books? No, a dozen pairs of underwear . . . and nothing else.

I looked at him. He looked back at me, shrugged his shoulders, and said, "Well, Mam always said make sure you have on clean underwear in case you ever get in an accident!"

Sometimes you have to find humor in the darkest places, and that was my one bright spot in this terrible situation! Fortunately, I knew at least one person to call. Many immigrants have no one. When you're an immigrant, the last thing you want to do is fail in the new country, and as irrational as it sounds, I felt as if my accident was a failure on my part. I will never forget the feeling of isolation as I lay in that hospital bed. Despite the care that I received from the doctors, nurses, and staff, I have never felt more alone in my life. In my darkest hours, I came to realize that I had to focus all my energies on picking myself up again. My accident meant that I had huge bills to pay and no way to do it. I had no one to turn to for help. Now, I wasn't looking for a handout or a bailout. It was up to me—I, and only I, needed to sort out this mess, and I knew it would take a long time. If I wanted to pay off my debts and go on to succeed, I was going to have to give 100-plus percent of my energy and effort to make it happen.

It turns out, it took me many years to dig myself out of the very deep financial hole caused by the accident. I worked night and day to meet my obligations and pay off my debts. I used to receive so many bills that sometimes I couldn't even bring myself to open them; I just stacked them up on the mantel. Whichever one fell from that pile onto the floor was the one that got paid first!

Looking back, the scars of that experience weren't just physical. One day, years later, my wife, Beverly, pointed out to me that I would never answer the house phone when it rang, even if it was right beside me. She asked me why this was. I had no idea at first. But then I thought about it and it came to me: Back when I was broke, I used to get calls from collection agencies at all hours of the day and night. Unbeknownst to me, this experience had filtered into my subconscious. The calls had impacted me so much that eventually I just stopped answering the phone. I didn't even know it, but years later, despite having achieved phenomenal success in my life, I still avoided picking up the phone when it rang! It just goes to show—the sense of isolation you feel as a stranger in a strange land lasts long after you have settled into your new home.

CHAPTER THREE

Disadvantage Three:

Immigrants Don't Have Many
Assets or Resources

Getting established in a new country means facing a series of diffi-cult challenges before you can acquire even the basics—challenges such as finding accommodations, transportation, and a job. These all require money and resources, and many people who come to this country are escaping poverty or hardship of some kind. Most of them don't have stacks of cash under their bed to bring with them.

I came to America with ninety-two dollars in my pocket. When I stepped off that plane, I had no idea how I was going to make it work. I just knew there was no other option.

NO SAFETY NET

When a tightrope artist steps off the platform and onto the wire, there's a safety net between him and the ground. Without that net, a fall would be catastrophic. For immigrants, there is no safety net—most have no significant assets or resources at their disposal. Many, like me, come here with the clothes on their back and less than $100 to their name. If they fall from their "wire," there's no one and nothing there to catch them. When you're operating in this environment, your mind-set is that there's no room for error—you can't put even one foot in the wrong place or you might topple and never recover. That can either drive you or it can cripple you.

NO ROOM FOR ERROR

Because there's no safety net, there's no room for mistakes. Nothing is predictable, and because you have limited resources, gambling on something that may not work is unthinkably risky. Everyday decisions that you would have made without much thought under normal circumstances in your home country are now mulled over and considered carefully because there's no leeway for error. From where you live to where you work to where you shop, you err on the side of caution. You can't afford to waste precious resources, so you're always looking for ways to save and budget every penny. This is why many immigrants live frugally and well below their means. And when they're able to establish enough savings, they begin sending money back to relatives overseas. These remittances are an incredibly important source of financial support to immigrants' families back home. According to the Pew Research Center, an estimated $582 billion was sent by immigrants to relatives in their home countries in 2015.

NO RICH UNCLE

It's often said that you need to spend money to make money. But for those who have to count every spare dime just to get by, that concept is just a fantasy. For immigrants, getting a loan to kick-start a business or make ends meet usually isn't possible. They are often shut out from lenders. Many don't even have a basic bank account.

For a few, there are other options. Some Korean immigrants, for example, use a system called *kye,* in which members contribute to a common savings pool and take turns borrowing. Some Latino communities have a similar system, known as *tanda* or *sociedad.* But many immigrants have no access to extra capital, unless it's of the sort offered by unscrupulous loan sharks who charge punishing rates of interest and take advantage of so many.

BRIAN'S STORY

Bungee Cord Blues

When I first started working in real estate, I didn't have a car. This is sort of a big deal when you're supposed to be driving clients to view homes! It became a running joke that when a prospective client asked me to take them to see some houses, I'd say, "Great. Why don't you drive, I'll navigate." That was my script, and I stuck to it!

On my first-ever listing appointment in National City, a friend of mine kindly loaned me his stepson's beat-up station wagon. This car had been in an accident and was driving on a wing and a prayer. There was even a bungee cord holding the door together! When you got to where you wanted to go, you had to do the limbo underneath the bungee cord, unhooking it but holding the top because you didn't want the door to fall off. Then, keeping the window open, you had to climb out, close the door, and hook up the bungee cord again. On the morning of my appointment, I drove this jalopy up to a house at the end of a cul-de-sac. I parked and did my whole song-and-dance routine of getting out of the car. A neighborhood kid stood watching me. He looked me up and down.

"Who are you?" he asked.

"I'm a real estate agent. I'm here to help list this family's home," I replied, trying to keep my dignity intact.

He went running through the doorway ahead of me, like the town crier.

"Hey, Mom!" he called. "The real estate man's here, and he's been in an accident!"

This was my MO for a very long time. I was the guy who always looked like he'd been in an accident! Living and working in such a frugal way didn't make me feel good, but I had to learn to cope with it. I couldn't run before I had learned to walk. Staying in sequence and working hard became my mantra for success. I took one day at a time, remembered all I had to be grateful for, remained humble, and kept my goals in sight. These days, I'm fortunate enough to travel all over the world in my own plane . . . but I still look back fondly on my days in that bungee-cord car because it taught me lessons about determination and hard work that I will carry with me for the rest of my life.

CHAPTER FOUR

Disadvantage Four:

Immigrants Don't Have Much Choice about Where They Start

LOW-LEVEL AND LOW-PAYING WORK

A few immigrants arrive here with superb educational qualifications and walk straight into top-level, high-paying jobs. But, as I've said, there are many others who come to these shores under very different circumstances. Their options are limited and, as a result, they're prepared to consider anything. They will do the sort of work that natives often reject. From washing dishes to painting houses, many immigrants start at the bottom by doing manual labor. Some of those jobs, such as mining, logging, construction, and farm work even present physical dangers. But when you're struggling and desperate, you will do whatever it takes to survive. And because the wages are low, working two or more jobs to make ends meet is a fact of life.

When I first came to California, I painted houses to pay the bills. Every morning I'd wait at the street corner where the contractors would go to hire people—mostly non-nationals—on a daily rate. It was backbreaking, low-paying employment, but it was work, and I was willing to do it. Years later, when I was a contractor myself, I made sure to go back to that same street corner and help others get a leg up. A person at the bottom may move up and gain success, but he or she should never forget what it felt like to be a stranger in a strange land, struggling to get started.

UNSOCIAL WORKING HOURS

Regular nine-to-five hours are a luxury that many immigrants don't get to enjoy. To get employment, they often settle for unsocial work hours and shifts that are grueling. Unfortunately, this takes its toll both physically and mentally. Studies have shown that the grind of these unsocial hours and conditions can have a serious effect on health, sleep, and family time, all adding to the stress that newcomers experience. But this is the collateral damage that immigrants pay to keep their heads above water.

STRESSFUL LIVING ENVIRONMENTS

Decent housing is expensive. It's difficult to meet that cost when you're working for low wages. It's no wonder that so many immigrants have less-than-ideal living arrangements—overcrowded, unhealthy, expensive . . . even dangerous. From sharing cramped housing with many others, to splitting the cost of rent, to being forced to occupy unsafe and unsanitary locations, immigrants face a host of challenges from the get-go. Unfortunately, this situation can often become a vicious cycle of poor living conditions, limited choices, and deteriorating health.

For newcomers, the path to homeownership is extremely challenging, and there are even more fences to jump and obstacles to face than there would be for natives:

- *Overcoming language barriers*: Understanding complicated and legally dense terms is difficult, even for those of us who are fluent in English. For non-English-speaking newcomers, conversations concerning real-estate transactions are far harder to conduct than the daily conversations they have at work or in the grocery store. The terminology can be complex and baffling.

- *Qualifying for a mortgage*: Lenders will generally look at U.S. credit history and tax returns, which means that those who are new to the country are at a serious disadvantage.

- *Getting co-op approval*: Housing discrimination based on national origin, race, or religion is illegal. However, boards that run cooperative buildings are entitled to evaluate potential buyers, and not all are well disposed to immigrants.

Despite these challenges, many immigrants still believe that buying a home and putting down roots is a critical part of the American

Dream—and many of them achieve this. According to a report by the Research Institute for Housing America, immigrants accounted for nearly 40 percent of the net growth in homeowners between 2000 and 2010, as compared to the 1970s, when they represented just over 5 percent of the growth.

BRIAN'S STORY

Faking It at Fotomat

When I first came here, I had many jobs that were low-paying. I painted houses, sold T-shirts at the beach, and worked night shifts to make ends meet. One of the most memorable jobs I had was at a Fotomat, which was a photo-development kiosk. I had absolutely zero experience, but somehow I managed to talk my way into the position. Let's just say I fudged my credentials! I'll always remember being shown what to do and bluffing my way through it, pretending that the equipment was a lot older than I was familiar with so I could cover up my ineptitude. It was a steep learning curve, and my first few hundred portraits were disastrous! While I worked at the Fotomat during the day, I was also studying for my real estate license and working as a security guard in a La Jolla motel at night. Like many immigrants, I juggled all of these commitments to get by. When you're really desperate and determined to succeed, that's what you do.

CHAPTER FIVE

Disadvantage Five:

Immigrants Don't Have Mentors or Role Models

What do the most successful people around us have in common? They seek the guidance of mentors. The definition of a *mentor* is an experienced and trusted adviser who provides guidance and training. In essence, mentors are people whose hindsight can become your foresight!

While they may have had a mentor connection in their own country, few immigrants have mentors or role models to turn to in their new home. It's not surprising that they run into difficulty because of this.

NOBODY TO TURN TO

As children, my brothers and I were mentored by my grandfather, Harry Buffini. A fourth-generation painter, Harry passed on his work principles to us. He taught us how to hold a brush and apply paint, how to patch and repair things, and even how to sweep the floor properly.

Two are better than one because they have a good return for their labor: If either of them falls down, one can help the other up. But pity anyone who falls and has no one to help them up.
—ECCLESIASTES 4:9–10 NLT

Most important, he taught us that every time we worked on a job, our good name was on the line. When I came to America, I initially had no mentor to turn to for advice, and I felt adrift because of it. When you've always had someone to go to for guidance and suddenly you don't, there's a void that leaves you vulnerable.

As a result, you can end up turning to the wrong people and getting some very bad advice.

NO TRACK TO RUN ON

When you've always lived a certain way, it can be a serious shock to your system when your lifestyle and surroundings abruptly change. It's as if the rug has been pulled out from under you—your regular and time-tested routines, habits, systems, and disciplines can disappear in a puff of smoke overnight. It's like running in a race on a paved track when, suddenly, the track slopes downhill and turns to sand and gravel. You have to adjust your stride to adapt to the different conditions, otherwise you could get injured. Your pace falters. You even trip and fall. You're in the race of your life, but you're no longer able to keep up. As everyone else starts passing you by, the winner's podium gets further and further out of reach.

NO SHOULDER TO LEAN ON

As the old song goes, "We all need somebody to lean on." For a stranger in a strange land, this is especially true.

When you're a newcomer to this country, you quickly learn that cultural nuances are plentiful. The true meanings of simple words and phrases can be lost in translation, and subtle differences in language, behavior, and humor can lead to misunderstandings.

Foreign ambassadors to a country usually travel with an official translator to help and guide them. Immigrants don't have the advantage of this type of shoulder to lean on and often have to learn things the hard way—by experience. Nonetheless, immigrants can help themselves settle in and go on to thrive if they tap into myriad other resources available to them. When I first came here, I couldn't believe the help I could access. I may not have had a physical shoulder to lean on, but in many other ways a lot of support was still available to me.

> *A shared joy is a double joy; shared sorrow is half a sorrow.*
> —SWEDISH PROVERB

For example, many of my mentors are people I have never even met, but I've read their books, watched their videos, listened to their tapes, and tapped into their online resources. In this way, I have learned from their wisdom and advice, just as if I had sat beside them and spent time in their company. Anyone can do this and reap the same rewards.

The fact is, many Americans don't know how fortunate they are that this culture is so open to personal growth. Today, even in some developed countries, these concepts are still relatively new. In many places, the idea of attending a personal growth seminar would be very strange indeed. Even in Ireland, where people are as hospitable and gracious as you'd find anywhere, there can be skepticism about this topic. But with a wealth of incredible resources at your fingertips, you would be foolish not to take advantage of them to grow and improve yourself.

BRIAN'S STORY

The Student of Success

When I arrived in America, I was very wet behind the ears. I had tons of ambition and drive, but I was like a rudderless boat adrift in a vast ocean—I had no clue what direction I was headed in. Gene Kullman is the man who changed that. A respected real estate agent, Gene took me under his wing and became my first mentor—and second father figure—in this new country. He taught me a lot about how to live and work here, which set me up for success.

I will never forget the day in 1989 when he took me to a seminar that featured all the great thought leaders and motivational speakers of the time, including Zig Ziglar, Jim Rohn, and Lou Holtz. For the first time, I was exposed to the personal growth and development world. This opened my eyes and showed me there were many ways to be mentored—America was light-years ahead in this regard. Back home in Ireland, no one had even heard of personal development!

> *Mentoring is a brain to pick, an ear to listen, and a push in the right direction.*
>
> JOHN C. CROSBY

Over time, I became a student of success. I began to read and study, devouring as much information as I possibly could about people who had achieved greatness in life. Over the years, I have been fortunate to become personal friends with some of my mentors. Other mentors I haven't met, but I've studied them from afar. Regardless, all of these people have helped me to grow and become the prosperous man I am today.

The Lens of Opportunity

The Natural Advantages of Immigrants

Introduction to Part Two

When the winds of change blow, some people build
walls and other people build windmills.

—CHINESE PROVERB

The difficulties and disadvantages that immigrants experience after arriving in America show just how much existing opportunity there is at a native's fingertips by comparison: Americans really do have a "leg up" on newcomers. The other side of the coin, though, shows that there are natural advantages immigrants have because they've left the comfort and familiarity of their homeland. Their natural advantages are actually what you can embrace to help you develop your own Emigrant Edge.

CHAPTER SIX

Advantage One:

Immigrants Are Coming to a Better Place

Immigrants risk everything for the chance of a new life in a better place. But when faced with the option of either staying where they are and struggling for the rest of their lives or moving to a land of opportunity and plenty, the best choice is often clear. While this new homeland is full of unknowns and challenges and devoid of friends and family, it is more appealing and a better prospect than remaining in a place that's so limited.

FREE AT LAST

The United States has become home to millions of immigrants, many of whom come here because they face social, political, or environmental repressions in their own country. In the land of their birth, they may not have the freedom to act, think, speak, or even worship as they want. In America, these freedoms are often taken for granted, but for immigrants who have endured the denial of even basic liberties, America represents the ultimate dream. Coming here offers life-changing opportunities to live and work in a place where they can finally realize their full potential and enjoy the inalienable rights to life, liberty, and the pursuit of happiness.

On a side note, many immigrants have defended these rights by serving in the military. It's estimated that in the American Civil War, 18 percent of the Union Army consisted of immigrants, most being from Germany and Ireland. Furthermore, of the exclusive group who have been awarded the Congressional Medal of Honor since 1861, 20 percent—or more than 700 soldiers—were immigrants. Today, America's military includes approximately 65,000 servicemen and -women born outside this country.

GOLD-PAVED STREETS

An Italian immigrant was once quoted as saying, "I came to America because I heard the streets were paved with gold. When I got here, I found out three things: First, the streets weren't paved with gold. Second, they weren't paved at all. Third, I was expected to pave them."

This saying reminds me of how I felt when I first came to this country! Back in Dublin, everyone thought America was a land of rich and plenty. TV shows like *Dallas* were very popular, so I assumed that everyone here lived that glamorous lifestyle. It was a bit of a shock to the system to realize that wasn't exactly the case!

While many immigrants will undoubtedly face economic hardship when they first get here, more often than not this country offers far better economic prospects than those they leave behind. In their home countries, there's no hope of doing any better than the generations that came before them. They are stuck in a depressing cycle of poverty and want. In America, people can dream. They can take economic initiative, serve others in the free market, and tap into their entrepreneurial spirit. Many immigrants take this opportunity and run with it.

According to Inc.com, immigrant entrepreneurs are most willing to take the risk of starting a business. In fact, the last recession would have been far worse without the growth of immigrant-owned businesses. From 1996 to 2011, according to the same website, the business start-up rate of immigrants increased by more than 50 percent, while the native-born start-up rate declined by 10 percent, to a thirty-year low. Despite accounting for only about 13 percent of the population, immigrants now start more than a quarter of new businesses in this country and are more than twice as likely to start a business as native-born citizens. These businesses are fast-growing too—over 20 percent of the 2014 Inc.com's 500 CEOs were immigrants. Their contribution to the American economy is undeniable: These companies pay approximately $126 billion in wages per year and employ one in ten Americans who work for private companies. In 2010, immigrant-owned businesses generated more than $775 billion in sales—a phenomenal figure.

THE SKY'S THE LIMIT

When an immigrant encounters opportunity that has so long been denied, it feels as if the sky is the limit. Suddenly, there's no cap on what you can achieve. Yes, there's hard work ahead, but the payoff is tremendous—the world is your oyster! This is the mind-set of the winning immigrant. It's how I felt when I stepped off that plane from Ireland all those years ago (once I got over the shock that I hadn't been magically transported to the set of *Dallas*!). It's incredible what you can achieve when you have that winning mind-set. Nothing and no one can stop you. Yes, it's stressful to have to start all over again, but not all stress is bad for you. It's all about perspective.

In a recent TED Talk, for example, Stanford University psychologist Kelly McGonigal explained that stress can be a friend. Yes, it can be crippling, but it can also be positive and a great motivator—and people who choose to believe that stress is good usually aren't affected negatively by it.

INSPIRATION

Russians in the Pacific Northwest

In *The Millionaire Next Door*, Dr. Thomas J. Stanley and Dr. William D. Danko outline a geographic, geonomic, and demographic overview of millionaires in America. According to their research, the number one ethnic group for becoming millionaires in this country in the past twenty years is Russians. It's hardly surprising. If you grow up in a culture that offers very little opportunity, and "the land of the free and the home of the brave" is willing to give you a chance at a new life, odds are you're going to do well.

It wasn't long ago that Russia was a communist country that oppressed its people. The government controlled all aspects of life—economic opportunity simply wasn't available for average citizens. So, when Russian immigrants flooded into this country to escape the repression, the closest landing site was the great state of Washington. When they got there, they very quickly discovered a unique business to which they could apply their talents—the American junkyard. Talk about a fish discovering water last! For most Americans, a junkyard is the last place they'd want to work, not the first place to get their start. But when you have the Emigrant Edge, you see opportunity where others see problems.

What did the Russians see? Americans wanted to get rid of their broken-down cars, so they disposed of them at the junkyard. Other Americans who wanted to repair their cars inexpensively needed a place to buy used parts. Our Russian friends saw a retail business with a zero cost of supply and a steady demand for sales. All they needed was to acquire the yard itself, and that's what many of them did. Today, many of these junkyard Russians are Washingtonian millionaires.

The truth is, nobody leaves a place where they already have everything they want. They leave because a new destination offers hope for a better life. A nonimmigrant can replicate this mind-set of wanting a better life by having a goal—a vision of and hope for a better place.

CHAPTER SEVEN

Advantage Two:

Immigrants Are Making a Fresh Start

Silent movie actress Mary Pickford once said, "You may have a fresh start any moment you choose, for this thing that we call 'failure' is not the falling down, but the staying down." Immigrants are starting over from scratch and this drives them forward. Natives can tap into this drive too. When they encounter failure or difficulty, they can always pick themselves back up, pledge not to stay down, and vow to begin again. I can tell you, I have personal experience with this. Once I got my feet on the ground in America, my first vocation was to become a real estate agent. Even though it wasn't all smooth sailing, I loved every minute of serving people and solving problems. There's no better feeling than handing a set of keys to someone who thought they'd never own a home, helping a family move into a bigger and better place, or freeing people from financial difficulty by selling a house that had become an anchor around their neck.

I did extremely well in real estate, and because of that, I was constantly being asked to come and speak at conferences to explain what I was doing and why it was successful. After doing that for a couple of years, I realized there was a huge need among people in the industry who were looking for systems to follow and how-tos to achieve success in real estate. It was at that time that my wife, Beverly, came and saw me speak at one of these conferences. She said, "Brian, you have a gift at this. I think you need to go and share with more people how to be successful in this business."

So we decided to pursue a new dream—to build a company called Providence Systems. We chose the name because, in the dictionary, *providence* is defined as God's providing and sustaining power of destiny. (We later had to change it to Buffini & Company because someone else had trademarked Providence Systems.)

It's an interesting thing that when you are preparing to make a fresh start with a new business, not everyone is on board. In this case, it was my own father who challenged me. He took me to one side and said, "Brian, you've become more successful than you ever imagined in real estate. Now you're going to be traveling all over the country speaking to people. Why don't you stay in the real estate business and do what you know how to do?"

I have tremendous respect for my dad, so I listened to what he had to say. However, something in my heart and gut was telling me I had to do this. I was 100 percent supported by Beverly, and I really felt joy in helping others. I knew that sharing the systems that had allowed me to succeed gave people clarity and hope for the same. So I went ahead, and for the next ten years the company grew at no less than 40 percent a year.

Ten years in, my father and I went for a coffee. He said to me, "Boy, I'm so glad you never listened to a word I said!"

Part of my joy in speaking is that not only have I experienced a fresh start as an immigrant, I have also experienced a fresh start as an American.

HIT THE RESET BUTTON

We're all familiar with the term *reboot* when it comes to computers. When your PC is giving you trouble—the screen freezes or a Word document disappears—you shut it down and restart it. When immigrants move to a new country, they reboot their life in much the same way. They wipe their slate clean, restart, and forge a new identity. We can all learn from this, whether we are immigrants or not.

Sometimes our lives get off track or stuck in a rut, and we need a jolt to bring us to our senses and help us get back on track again. When this happens, it doesn't mean you have to change everything about your life. When you reboot a computer, you're not replacing the core operating system, you're just eliminating the components that are inhibiting its function and setting it up for optimal performance. If your computer is slow and sluggish, of course you do what you can to make it operate with more speed and efficiency.

It's the same with life. Instead of getting bogged down or frustrated because you're repeating old patterns and not getting very far, you can reboot, refresh, even upgrade to a new plan. It's always okay to take a step back to reevaluate your circumstances. You are free to reinvent yourself.

NO LONGER A PRISONER OF THE PAST

The experiences from our past can shape our lives and help us make sense of the present. But when events from your past are painful, they can have a negative effect on your personal growth and development. When you move away from the country of your birth, the grip that the chains of your former life have on you is loosened. When an immigrant comes to a new country, in a sense he or she can shed themselves of their past, like a snake sheds its skin.

Never be a prisoner of your past. Become the architect of your future.
—ROBIN SHARMA

Instead of concentrating on their painful past, they can now focus on new goals and circumstances, while drawing from lessons they've already learned. This allows them to see adversity as opportunity in disguise.

We can all learn from this wisdom: cutting the chains, breaking free of the past, and focusing on the here and now is vital for advancing on the path to success. It's all about keeping a forward-looking perspective. Allowing yourself to start over is like mentally turning the page and beginning your story again, writing a new script on a blank screen. As clinical psychologist and author Dr. Henry Cloud said at one of our events, "You're not doomed because of your past—you can always get a new one."

NEW BEGINNING = HOPE

Life can be difficult. When you're a stranger in a strange land, it can be even more so. As I've been sharing, there are many obstacles to overcome and challenges to face when you're trying to create a new life for yourself. That's why hope is so important to an immigrant. If you don't have hope that

The past is a foreign country: they do things differently there.
—L. P. HARTLEY

you will one day accomplish your dreams, you have nothing.

But being hopeful isn't just having optimism that everything will turn out okay even if the odds are stacked against you. There's actually a science to hope.

Psychologist Charles R. Snyder devised the Hope Theory in 1991. According to this theory, hopeful people tackle problems with a particular mind-set. They have the will and determination to achieve their goals, but they also have a set of *strategies* to do so. Hope isn't just a feel-good emotion; it's a dynamic cognitive motivational system. Those who are truly hopeful plan how to achieve their goals and they monitor their progress so they don't go off track. If they fail, they don't quit because they have hope that they will succeed. Hopeful people never stop learning.

INSPIRATION

The Lost Boy of Africa

One of the most powerful stories of hope that I have ever read was about Legson Kayira, a "Lost Boy" of Africa. Kayira was born in a small, impoverished village in Malawi. Soon after his birth, his mother felt she had no option other than to throw him into the Didimu River because she couldn't afford to feed him.

Kayira was rescued, but it's hard to imagine how anyone could recover from such a traumatic experience at the beginning of life. But as C.S. Lewis once wrote, "Hardships often prepare ordinary people for an extraordinary destiny." Kayira was destined for an extraordinary life.

After completing his secondary education, Kayira was hungry to learn more. He decided the only way to further his learning was to travel to America. He had read many books about America in school and, inspired by Abraham Lincoln and Booker T. Washington, he decided this was where he could have his freedom and independence. Kayira was penniless, so the only way for him to get to the "land of the free" was to walk. Amazingly, that's exactly what he did! He set off on this epic journey barefoot, carrying his only possessions: food, an ax, and two books. He traveled like this for thousands of miles through the African bush and across four countries. Most people would have given up, but Kayira had hope and, more than that, he developed a plan.

Braving harsh conditions and dangers like lions, hyenas, and snakes, he walked through Malawi, Tanzania, Uganda, and Sudan. In the library in Khartoum, Kayira found a directory of American universities and chose the first one to catch his eye—Skagit Valley College in Mount Vernon, Washington. He filled out an application, sent it in, and was awarded a scholarship. On hearing this news, the good people of Skagit Valley raised the money to help him get to America.

It took Kayira two years to get to Washington. Once there, he earned a political science degree and then went on to achieve remarkable success by becoming a graduate student at Cambridge University and the author of several novels. His autobiography *I Will Try* was on the *New York Times* bestseller list for sixteen weeks after its publication in 1965 and was translated into many languages. All this from a boy who had the worst possible start in life!

So, you see, hope is much more than simply a powerful emotion. When combined with grit, determination, and a plan, there's no limit to where you can go or what you can achieve.

CHAPTER EIGHT

Advantage Three:

Immigrants Are Pursuing Their Dreams

There's nothing more powerful than a dream! Having a dream is vital to success. If you can see it, you can achieve it. When immigrants leave everything they know behind, they keep their dream of success uppermost in their mind. Nonimmigrants must do the same.

THE AMERICAN DREAM

Ask six people to define the American Dream and you'll get six different answers: financial well-being, personal freedom, educational opportunities, home ownership, a better life, and opportunity for their children. The American Dream represents different things to different people.

To an immigrant, the core of the Dream is always the same: the ability to earn a better life in a free market and pass on even greater opportunity to the next generation. What marks the most successful immigrants is their ability to doggedly work toward achieving their dreams, regardless of the obstacles they meet along the way. By adopting this mind-set, anyone can tap into the same energy and motivation.

THE AMERICAN WAY

Just what is the American Way? According to Webster, it's "a method or manner of behaving or living that is regarded as distinctively characteristic of the U.S. and representative of its values."

American author William Herberg offers the following definition:

> The "American Way of Life" is individualistic, dynamic, and pragmatic. It affirms the supreme value and dignity of the individual; it stresses incessant activity on his part, for he is never to rest but is always to be striving to "get ahead"; it defines an ethic of self-reliance, merit, and character, and judges by achievement: "deeds, not creeds" are what count. The "American Way of Life" is humanitarian, "forward-looking," optimistic. Americans are easily the most generous and philanthropic people in the world, in terms of their ready and unstinting response to suffering anywhere on the globe. The American believes in progress, in self-improvement, and quite

fanatically in education. But above all, the American is idealistic. Americans cannot go on making money or achieving worldly success simply on its own merits; such "materialistic" things must, in the American mind, be justified in "higher" terms, in terms of "service" or "stewardship" or "general welfare." . . . And because they are so idealistic, Americans tend to be moralistic; they are inclined to see all issues as plain and simple, black and white, issues of morality.*

I believe this statement still holds true today, more than half a century after it was written. The American way of life is different from other countries' because this nation was formed under very different belief and value systems than other lands. As national archivist John W. Carlin wrote in the National Archives and Records Administration's 1999 Annual Report, "We are different because our government and our way of life are not based on the divine right of kings, the hereditary privileges of elites, or the enforcement of deference to dictators. They are based on pieces of paper, the Charters of Freedom—the Declaration that asserted our independence, the Constitution that created our government, and the Bill of Rights that established our liberties."

Part of this country's appeal to those not born here is a special spirit unique to this land that is difficult to analyze, define, or explain. This spirit, this American Way, is at the heart of what attracts so

---

* William Herberg, *Protestant, Catholic, Jew: An Essay in American Religious Sociology* (Chicago: University of Chicago Press, 1983).

many to these shores. The American Way isn't the only way, of course, but it is a way that shines as a beacon of hope and light to millions all over the globe.

THE AMERICAN GUARANTEE

The Will Smith movie *The Pursuit of Happyness* is one of my favorite films. The film is based on the amazing true story of Chris Gardner, who was once a guest speaker at one of Buffini & Company's events. A prodigy in scientific research, Gardner came to San Francisco as a young man ready and eager to make his mark on the world. While there, he set his sights on the fiercely competitive world of high finance. He secured an entry-level position at a prestigious firm, but, unfortunately, he soon became trapped by a set of circumstances—a perfect storm of trouble—that left him homeless and with a toddler son to care for. He and his son spent almost a year on the street—sleeping in shelters, getting food from soup lines, and even spending a night in the public restroom of a subway station. Determined never to give up and despite all the odds, Gardner eventually went on to build a fortune on Wall Street. Today, he's a renowned entrepreneur, investor, stockbroker, motivational speaker, author, and philanthropist. His story is the very essence of the American Dream, but it also portrays that a dream is not enough unless it's supported by a specific set of goals and the relentless hope needed to achieve them.

It's said that Benjamin Franklin once declared that the Constitution only guarantees you the right to *pursue* happiness—happiness is not handed to you on a silver platter. You have to catch your happiness yourself. We all know there are no guarantees in life, no sure things. There are always unexpected twists and turns, ups and downs that obstruct, detain, and sometimes get you off track. But if you have a clear set of goals, you're more likely to stay the course and not give up. Goals are the oxygen of dreams; without them, your dreams will stay just that—dreams.

INSPIRATION

The Power of Dreams and Goals

G oals are the targets you set to turn your dreams into reality. They give you focus, help you measure progress, keep you on track, help you to overcome procrastination, and keep you motivated. However, you must be specific and realistic. Study the following two charts, and then write down your long-term and short-term goals and review them often.

Begin with the end in mind.
—STEPHEN R. COVEY

You must also be patient. Successful immigrants know that progress takes time. They're prepared to work for years to become an overnight success! Likewise, you have to commit to a system and be steadfast. Track your activities over time so you can see your progress. This will help you stay motivated and maintain a positive attitude.

THE POWER OF
DREAMS & GOALS

The **5 STEPS** of
Goal Setting

Likely
SUCCESS RATE

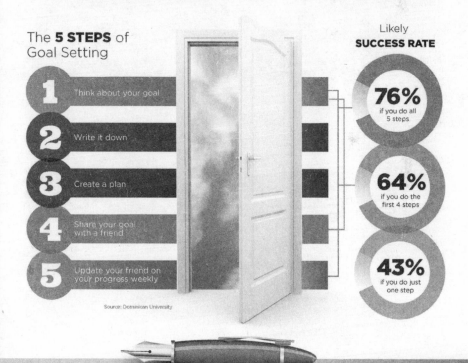

1 Think about your goal

2 Write it down

3 Create a plan

4 Share your goal with a friend

5 Update your friend on your progress weekly

Source: Dominican University

76%
if you do all
5 steps

64%
if you do the
first 4 steps

43%
if you do just
one step

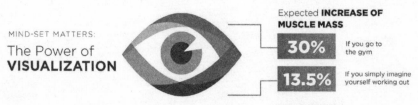

Why is it important to *Write down your goals?*
You'll internalize them and expect to achieve them.

Source: Ferguson & Sheldon

MIND-SET MATTERS:
The Power of
VISUALIZATION

Expected **INCREASE OF MUSCLE MASS**

30% If you go to the gym

13.5% If you simply imagine yourself working out

Source: Psychology Today

Top 3 **EMOTIONAL BENEFITS** of Achieving Goals

1 Joy **2** Pride **3** Motivation

Source: Kreibig, Gendolla & Scherer, Deci & Ryan

Top 3 **STRUCTURAL BENEFITS** of Goal Setting

1 Increased organization **2** Prioritized tasks **3** Managed intentions

Source: Shah & Kruglanski

RANDOM STATS

40% Americans that make New Year's resolutions

25% that abandon their New Year's resolutions after one week

60% that abandon their New Year's resolutions within six months

70% of teenagers set goals for themselves

92% of high school and college students are working on a goal

Source: *Forbes*, Michael Hyatt, Ba & Wang, StageofLife.com

CHAPTER NINE

Advantage Four:

Immigrants Know about Sacrifice

Having to leave the country of your birth is a brutal price to pay for a dream. It takes a toll emotionally, physically, spiritually, and relationally. On the plus side, knowing and understanding the sacrifice it takes to pursue your dream is a real advantage. If you know what it takes, you can *do* what it takes.

People often say to me that they'd love to do what I do. Yes, I do live an exciting and fulfilling life, but take it from me, it isn't glamorous! I've spent countless exhausting days on the road, crisscrossing the country. I've spent hundreds of nights in tiny hotel rooms with bad addresses and even worse accommodations. I have arrived at venues in the middle of nowhere to find two people waiting to hear me speak . . . and one of those was the next speaker! While on the road, I've missed family events, sports occasions, birthdays, and anniversaries. I now have more balance in my life, but there's no denying that when I was getting established, those first years were tough. That's why when people say to me, "I wish I could be you," I sometimes reply, "Are you crazy?!"

The thing is, I was prepared to do the tough work because I knew there was a price to be paid for success. As the Chinese general, military strategist, and philosopher Sun Tzu wrote in *The Art of War,* "Victory is reserved for those who are willing to pay its price." You can't have victory if you don't pay a price.

Success doesn't come easy, and it doesn't come free. Once you accept that fact, the hard work you do and the sacrifices you make are nonnegotiable—they're an expected part of the journey.

PAIN FUELS

We've already touched on the pain of leaving your loved ones behind when you leave your home country. This pain can cut like a knife, and it never leaves you; but it can also drive and motivate you. Pain can be fuel. When you know what you're giving up to make it in your new world, you know that, come hell or high water, you'd better make it work! Otherwise, your suffering will be for nothing.

> *When everything seems to be going against you, remember the plane takes off against the wind, not with it.*
> —HENRY FORD

SECURITY BLANKET

When my son Alex was a baby, he had a security blanket that never left his side. Everywhere we went, "blankie" would come with us.

In the car, to church, at the mall, in bed—that blanket was his constant companion and he refused to let it go. We couldn't even get it from him to wash it! We had to wait until he fell asleep and then sneak into his room to kidnap it, wash it, and put it back before he woke up.

Feeling safe is a primal need. Our "blankie" can take many forms—family, friends, community, steady income, or money in the bank. Whatever it is, if it's taken away from us, we have two choices: We can move forward, accepting that we have suffered a loss, or we can stay stuck where we are, forever defined by what we have lost.

Successful immigrants lose their security blanket when they leave home, but they still move forward and step out into the new world, always looking ahead. They don't forget where they came from, but they learn new coping mechanisms and new ways to proceed without the support and comfort of what they once relied upon. Doing this takes a lot of courage and grit, qualities that will get anyone far in life.

IDENTITY THEFT

We've all heard stories of identity theft. Probably the most famous is that of Frank Abagnale, who was played by Leonardo DiCaprio in the 2002 movie *Catch Me if You Can*. Abagnale evaded authorities by posing as various characters, including an airline pilot, a doctor, and a history professor, all while committing approximately $4 million worth of fraud. Eventually, he was caught and convicted. (By the way, he was later hired by the FBI as an expert on forgery and document theft and went on to start a business to educate others on how to avoid becoming a fraud victim.)

But identity theft can also take on other, unexpected forms. It can mean that you go from a place of knowledge to a place of ignorance.

I've been blessed to have met many fascinating people during my life. Some of them are famous figures in the public eye, but many are private individuals who have had just as much impact on me. One of these is a Serbian man who has helped build some of the homes that my family and I have lived in.

The first time I met this man, he was painting my kitchen. We got to talking and he told me that, before he came to America, he was the head of the entire train system back in his home country of Serbia. Well, that revelation just about blew me away. Honestly, I felt uncomfortable about it. This man was way overqualified to do the kind of work he was doing for me, and I told him so. But he had a very different attitude.

"Brian," he said, "I'm happy to do this work. Maybe I won't do it forever, but I enjoy the challenge of learning and perfecting new skills. Besides, it's getting me to where I want to go."

Well, I thought his gracious attitude was just phenomenal, and it opened my eyes. His identity was being changed from a man of position in the workforce to that of a manual laborer, but he was rolling with it. His perspective showed that he saw these changes as positive, not negative. He was right to think this way. When you reinvent yourself, there's no room for shame or apology. If you're moving toward where you want to be, you should hold your head up high and be proud!

INSPIRATION

The Cuban Boxer

Years ago I held a Buffini & Company Master-Mind Summit® event at the MGM Grand Hotel in Las Vegas and brought Neil Armstrong in as a guest speaker. While we were waiting backstage, I met a facilities supervisor who was moving trash cans and Dumpsters around. I was immediately struck by his physical presence. He had these giant, muscular shoulders and a very tiny waist. He was the picture of health and fitness. But it wasn't just his physical appearance that struck me—his smile lit up the room.

As we prepared to go onstage, I kept glimpsing him out of the corner of my eye and catching snippets of his unusual accent. So I asked him where he was from. It turned out he was from Cuba. I knew this man had a story to tell . . . but he wasn't ready to share it with me.

Over the course of the next four or five days, I chased him down every chance I could. Eventually, he spoke to me. It turned out this man was a champion boxer who had once competed in the Olympics. To escape great poverty and destitution, he, his brother, and his two best friends built a raft to cross the shark-infested waters to America. They had no water or food for two weeks—and he was the only one who made it. Talk about paying a price to get here. That sort of experience would crush many of us. But this guy had a different attitude. He had sacrificed everything to make it to the land of the free, and he was making the most of it. Here was a boxing champ in the back of the MGM Grand Hotel moving trash cans around. But he considered himself blessed to be doing it, even after everything he had suffered during his life.

I was so impressed by this man that I tried to hire him. But the general manager of the hotel wouldn't hear of it. He told me, "He's the best I've got. I've got plans for him." Everyone recognized what a special person he was. He was set to achieve his dreams when he left Cuba, all because of his spirit of gratitude and his positive, hardworking attitude. He had experienced enormous adversity, but he had refused to be beaten by it. Instead, he used it to keep moving forward and growing.

My brother Dermot always says, "We become successful in life by overcoming adversity, so why do we try to remove it from our children's lives?"

Isn't that so true? If we wrap our children in cotton and protect them from every knock and scrape, they won't ever develop the grit and guts they need to survive and thrive when they encounter difficulties, like that champion Cuban boxer. As Albert Einstein said, "Adversity introduces a man to himself."

So, even if you're sweeping the floor or cleaning dishes, you need to develop that spirit. If you have gratitude and energy in your dealings with others, believe me, people take notice. Don't focus on the difficulties you encounter. Focus on the fact that you're in the game.

CHAPTER TEN

Advantage Five:

Immigrants Have the Edge

FOCUS

There's a really clever acronym for FOCUS: Follow One Course Until Successful. This explains exactly what focus is and should be—a path that you follow doggedly until you reach your final destination . . . success!

Focus is supremely important when working toward a goal. No matter how much talent or energy you have, if you don't focus on a particular target you'll more than likely get distracted, lose your momentum, and never realize your full potential or achieve all that you're capable of. As Bruce Lee once said, "The successful warrior is the average man with laser-like focus."

Successful immigrants have supreme focus. They know what they want, lock in on it, and take off. They have a target and this is always at the forefront of their mind. Their eyes are always on the prize.

NO PLAN B

When I was a young boy, my mother used to tell me, "Necessity is the mother of invention." By this she meant that, even if I didn't have everything I wanted, I should be inventive with what I'd been given and make the best of it. I'm sure she didn't realize at the time just how much those words would affect my ability to flourish in another country. Other immigrants are in exactly the same position to apply this concept—instead of seeing their disadvantages as a negative, they can make them work in their favor. Immigrants have no plan B, so plan A has to work! Having no plan B means you don't give up by allowing yourself any excuses. Sticking with one plan or course of action enables you to devote all of your energy, time, and passion with ultimate focus.

Lack of direction, not lack of time, is the problem. We all have twenty-four-hour days.
—ZIG ZIGLAR

Of course, there will be ups and downs, anxieties, and worries, but as Scripture says, "If you are faithful in little things, you will be faithful in large ones" (Luke 16:10 NLT). Sometimes you have to believe that if you're being faithful to what you need to do to be successful and if you stay patient while sticking to your plan, then the dots will eventually connect. Steve Jobs once said, "You can't connect the dots looking forward; you can only connect them looking backward. So you have to trust that the dots will somehow connect in your future. . . . This approach has never let me down, and it has made all the difference in my life."

DO THE HUSTLE

When we think of the term *hustle,* many of us visualize something negative. But to hustle doesn't always mean that you're doing something shady or unsavory—there can also be very positive connotations. If you're hustling, it means you're not prepared to rest on your laurels and wait for Lady Luck to shine on you. It means you're focused on your goals, doing what it takes to reach them and not allowing the word *can't* into your vocabulary. In business, hustling means taking action, being proactive with your client base, and promoting and selling with passion.

In a new world, immigrants have to hustle just to keep their heads above water. Those who go on to achieve success have developed the knack of keeping their eyes open for opportunity. Hustlers aren't satisfied unless they're moving forward and accomplishing something. They subscribe to the Nike "Just Do It"® mentality of initiative and hard work.

BRIAN'S STORY

An Unwise Investment

I've had many great successes in my life, but I've also had many great failures and disappointments. As Winston Churchill once said, "Success consists of going from failure to failure without loss of enthusiasm." How true that is.

One of my most significant failures was an investment that went terribly wrong. At the time, I was doing really well in my career and was one of the most successful real estate agents in the country. I was looking for an investment for the money I had made, and I came across a company that manufactured hand-held air cooling appliances. I was immediately sold on these misting units—as an Irishman, I'd never fully adapted to the hot and sunny California weather, and these little appliances really helped to cool me down. I poured a lot of money into this company, convinced I was going to make a fortune.

The investment went well at first—the cooler fans were a new and exciting product, and they sold like blazes in the Southwest. But when we branched out to other regions, sales started to drop off the face of the earth. Turns out, the mister was perfect for dry heat . . . but not so good for the sort of humid air conditions you get in other states. I hadn't done my research properly and, boy, did I pay for it. Long story short, I ended up losing $2.9 million. It was everything my wife and I had. That year, we couldn't even buy a turkey for Christmas dinner. I felt like a complete failure.

So I was down and out for a while, but I rallied again—I refused to declare defeat. Instead, I went back to the hard-work principles I had applied before the bust. There was no plan B, so in my mind it was sink or swim and I was determined to swim—I would pull my family out of the mess I'd gotten us into. I gained a new sense of determination. I had already succeeded in the past, so I knew I could do it again. I buckled down, hustled, and worked like never before. It took awhile, but I slowly made the journey back to financial health and stability.

> *The ultimate measure of a man is not where he stands in moments of comfort and convenience, but where he stands at times of challenge and controversy.*
>
> MARTIN LUTHER KING, JR.

Maybe it's no surprise that my family teases me that I'm like the guy in the Chumbawamba song . . . when I get knocked down, I get back up again! Well, that's because, in my mind, I have no choice. When you're a successful immigrant, you are all in because you have to be. There's no safety net or backup plan.

This is the focused and driven mind-set needed to succeed in business or anything else, no matter where you come from.

By the way, you don't have to be in a place of hardship to have a determined mind-set. I'll never forget a man who once approached me and said, "You know, Brian, you came to America with ninety-two dollars. You were only here a short time when you got run over by a car. You were rushed to the hospital, had thirteen surgeries, and ended up two hundred and fifty thousand dollars in debt. All those experiences gave you this motivation and drive."

I had to agree that all those bad things had, unfortunately, happened to me.

Then he said, "You know, I grew up in a loving home. I went to school, I got good grades, and I did well in college. I've just never been motivated because nothing bad has ever happened to me."

"All right," I replied. "How about you and me go out to the parking lot? I'll run over you a couple of times, backward and forward if you like. That'll get you motivated in no time!" Of course, I was just kidding around, but here's the thing: You don't need to be run over to get fired up about pursuing a dream—you just need some fresh perspective to realize how lucky you really are.

When immigrants come to this country, they have to contend with many disadvantages. These disadvantages—so challenging for them—are your advantages if you happen to have been born here. Immigrants also have some natural advantages that help to give them an edge when they get here. You can learn and acquire all of them. It's within your power—just step back and gain some perspective.

Analyze your own history and the history of your predecessors, and then ask yourself what they would have done with your opportunities if they were in your shoes right now. Would they focus on what they don't have or would they be overjoyed with what they do? The Emigrant Edge is in you—somewhere in your DNA, from someone in your family who possessed all of these qualities—so tap into that power and realize the opportunities you have in front of you.

In the next section, we're going to explore the seven traits of successful immigrants. Adopting these traits will enable you to access the power of the Emigrant Edge in your own life.

PART THREE

WHAT IS THE EDGE?

The Seven Traits of Successful Immigrants

Introduction to Part Three

The essence of America—that which really unites us—
is not ethnicity, or nationality or religion—it is an idea—and what an idea
it is: That you can come from humble circumstances and do great things.

CONDOLEEZZA RICE

George Santayana, author and philosopher, once said, "Those who cannot remember the past are doomed to repeat it." This is so true. When we ignore history's lessons, we're vulnerable to repeat its failures, but what happens when we forget our history's *greatness*?

The fabric of this country is composed of countless inspiring stories of people who came here and built fortunes and raised families. Those folks arrived with nothing and battled and fought to make a better life for themselves, no matter the odds. Along the way, they exhibited consistent traits and patterns that ensured their success. They developed many of these traits either through the pain of trial and error or by modeling someone they admired.

Our history's past can be our path to a better future. Like many people, I have a curiosity and a thirst for knowledge about the past. I love researching my family tree. Of course, there's only so far back I can dig before I hit a dead end. But even though I may not have all the information needed to see the full picture of my heritage, I know that who I am today is the result of actions taken and lessons learned by my ancestors. Think about it: Chances are, if you take the time to research your family history, you'll discover that your predecessors were immigrants too. I encourage you to do this—find out where your ancestors originated. Discover what traits they had and the culture they brought with them to this country. Imagine what they would have done with the opportunities you now have! Through many years of my own study, I've discovered that all successful immigrants possess seven key traits. These traits, although generations old, are still as applicable and relevant in today's world as they were in our forefathers' time. These are the seven traits of the Emigrant Edge. They will resonate with natives at a deep level too, because somewhere in your DNA and bloodline is someone who exhibited some or all of these traits. Imitate them in your own life and you will be equipped to thrive and succeed.

> *The voice of the ancestor brings enlightenment.*
> —KOREAN PROVERB

CHAPTER ELEVEN

Trait One:

A Voracious Openness to Learn

A voracious openness to learn is probably the number one prerequisite for success. As Elie Wiesel—Auschwitz survivor, Nobel Prize winner, and immigrant—said, "There is divine beauty in learning. . . . Others have been here before me, and I walk in their footsteps."

Successful people don't achieve in solitary confinement or in a vacuum. They go out of their way to meet others, have new experiences, and learn about different aspects of life. They have a constant drive to want to know more—one new discovery leads to another. They aren't satisfied to learn one thing and then stop. As an old saying goes, "If you're not willing to learn, no one can help you. If you are determined to learn, no one can stop you!"

When I first arrived in America as an almost penniless teenager, I very quickly discovered that trying to get by on my own achieved nothing . . . I got nowhere. With no one and nothing to support or guide me, I floundered. But as I've already said, thanks to my first mentor, Gene Kullman, I realized there were many incredible resources at my fingertips—all I had to do was tap into them. That is when I began to study and imitate successful people who had gone before me. It wasn't rocket science—I learned what they had done to succeed, and then I found a way to apply it to my own life and circumstances.

I can honestly say that a voracious openness to learn has been a key to my success. A desire to grow—the humility to ask for, receive, and implement advice and then share with others what I've learned—has done more for me and my success than any zeros accumulated in a bank account.

I have discovered that finding your life's work is a process of elimination, not selection. You discover what you don't like long before you ever find what you love. Then you find a need connected to what you enjoy and fill that need in such a way that is better than your competition.

Because I applied what I learned over the years and recognized that people needed direction and clarity in achieving their own success, Buffini & Company was born. It is now the number one small-business coaching and training company in the U.S. From small acorns, mighty oaks grow! I teach many things at my seminars, but one of the most important is this lesson: Be a voracious learner. As I discuss this concept, many people can remember their parents and grandparents saying the same thing over the years. It's a timeless principle, tried and tested by those who have preceded us.

Having a voracious openness to learn requires three things:

1. YOU GOTTA BE "HONGRY"

My friend, the author and motivational speaker Les Brown, is one of the most inspirational people I know. Les is on a continual quest to pass on knowledge, and it's a quest he imbues with so much fun you don't even know you're learning! He has often said to me in his wonderfully rich Southern accent, "Brian, you gotta be hongry." What does he mean? Simply put, you must ask yourself what you're going to do today so that you have a brighter future tomorrow. Are you hungry to learn and improve? Hungry enough to reinvent yourself, grow beyond your present circumstances, make no excuses, get up again even if you're knocked down, and work harder than you ever have before for your dreams?

I love this message and know for a fact that it's true. If you want to make the most of life, you can't settle for the status quo. Surviving doesn't bring the same fulfillment as thriving. In order to thrive you have to be alert, open, ready for new possibilities, and on the lookout for ways to grow and get better. As legendary football coach Lou Holtz told me, "If you're not growing, you're dying." You must have that fire in your belly—the desire to learn and improve—and the belief that you have greatness within. The most successful immigrants have this in spades.

Take the world-famous philanthropist Andrew Carnegie, for example. Carnegie was an immigrant from Scotland who came to America in the 1800s and, driven by a hunger inside, built a steel empire worth millions.

Like many immigrants before and after him, he started with nothing. As a teenager, he worked as a bobbin boy in a textile mill.

He was determined to improve his lot in life, but he couldn't afford to buy books to study or even pay the two-dollar subscription for a local library. But he didn't let that stop him! Undeterred, he wrote to the library asking for access. When he was refused, he went to court and got the ruling overturned. He was only seventeen, but he was on his way to a lifetime of learning.

Years later, after he had become the richest man in the world, Carnegie donated $60 million to fund a system of 1,689 public libraries across America. After his early experiences, he believed that learning should no longer be just for the wealthy elite but open to everyone from every walk of life, rich or poor, young or old. This idea that libraries should be public and free was a revolutionary one back then—and one we still benefit from today. Many of these libraries remain the most beautiful public spaces in towns all across this country.

> *Man is what he reads.*
> —JOSEPH BRODSKY

2. YOU NEED A "JUST DO IT!"® MIND-SET

We all know people who are all talk. They like to tell you what they're going to do and how they're going to do it, but they don't ever get around to it! Now, as an Irishman, talking is in my blood. When I get together with my siblings and my parents, the noise level goes through the roof as we compete with one another to tell stories and make everyone laugh. As we say back home, we could talk the hind legs off a donkey. None of us is ever stuck for an opinion, and we believe everyone else is entitled to hear it!

But, even though talking is definitely good for you on many levels, it can't be *all* you do. Those who want to succeed in life certainly can't be all talk and no action. At some point they have to, as they say, grab the bull by the horns and really *go* for it! *Action* is what matters most for reaching goals.

> *Talk doesn't cook rice.*
> —CHINESE PROVERB

Remember the tin man from *The Wizard of Oz*? When he stopped moving, he seized up and got stuck—literally and metaphorically. It's the same for us—if we don't keep in motion by learning, growing, and moving forward, we can become rigid and set in our ways. If you're not moving, you're not growing.

It isn't what we say or think that defines us—it's what we do. *Actions* speak louder than words. Successful people spend time dreaming of what they want in life, just like everyone else. The difference between them and people who don't succeed, however, is that after they dream, they then take action steps to make that dream a reality. They face the change and uncertainty in front of them, instead of shrinking from it. They view disappointments and hurdles not as failures, but as opportunities to learn and refine themselves. They know that there is never a more perfect time to do anything than now. There's no overthinking anything, no waiting until all their ducks are in a row. They don't just talk the talk, they walk the walk.

> *Even if you're on the right track, you'll get run over if you just sit there.*
> —WILL ROGERS

So, next time you're tempted to talk instead of do, think of the world-famous Nike ad "Just Do It!" Stop talking about it, quit procrastinating, and just get up and go!

3. YOU MUST COMMIT TO C.A.N.I.
(CONSTANT AND NEVER-ENDING IMPROVEMENT)

People often call me a "self-made" man, but that isn't true. I'm not self-made—I'm a product of parenting, mentoring, personal development, and coaching. In short, I'm an ordinary man living an extraordinary life because I was willing to grow and improve.

I've already mentioned that, as a young boy growing up in Dublin, I had no clue about personal growth and development. I was hungry to learn and ambitious to succeed and my parents always encouraged me to be the best that I could be. But it wasn't until after I came to America that I was exposed to a whole new world of learning that I'd never known existed. I had no idea what the term *self-improvement* even meant, but my mind-set quickly shifted when I got here. I started to soak up all the wisdom and knowledge available to me, and I realized that, instead of wishing life was easier, I had to make *myself* better. The idea that you need to work harder on yourself than on your job was an unusual concept for a young Irish lad to understand, but once I did, it sure worked out well!

Formal education will make you a living. Self-education will make you a fortune.
—JIM ROHN

Today, I'm proud to say I'm a student of success. Reading books like Dale Carnegie's *How to Win Friends and Influence People* and Napoleon Hill's *Think and Grow Rich* shifted my worldview. Then I moved on to Norman Vincent Peale, Og Mandino, Zig Ziglar, Jim Rohn, Stephen Covey, and Lou Tice. Studying what these motivational thought leaders had to say turned on a lightbulb over my head. Suddenly, all the content I'd been absorbing clicked with me. I now had the help I needed and knew how and where to channel my desires and energy to become a better person and accomplish great things. I began to improve myself and grow as a person by listening to countless audiotapes and reading hundreds of books. These resources became my constant companions, and as a result, everything—my faith, my relationships, my business, and my career—changed for me.

The C.A.N.I. principle of Constant And Never-ending Improvement is one I live by to this day. I learned from the great Jim Rohn that you can't change the sea, soil, rain, sunshine, or the seasons, but you can work on your philosophy, language, attitude, personality, communication, and abilities. This is what I try passionately to do— and it's all thanks to the trailblazers who have gone before and inspired me. I have an insatiable appetite for knowledge, and my natural curiosity means I'm always eager to learn new things, explore new ideas, and have new experiences. I'll never learn the meaning of "enough"—there's no such thing. I believe that the world is an endlessly fascinating place and we're blessed to live in an age where knowledge is so easily accessible. If we want to know more about any subject under the sun, all we have to do is read a book or listen to a tape. (If you're a Millennial reading this, Google what a cassette tape is!) Imagine what our ancestors would have done with the opportunities we have. Would they have tried to learn as much as they possibly could about the world, or would they have watched endless, useless online videos that do nothing more than sap time and energy?

I may not have a string of letters after my name, but I still consider myself to be very well educated because of the experiences I have had, the books I have read, and the study I have done over the years. What I have learned along the way is that if you work hard on yourself—by honing your skills and improving your talents—nothing can hold you back from becoming great.

If you take a tour through Buffini & Company today, you'll see the Jim Rohn Conference Room, the Zig Ziglar Conference Room, the Lou Tice Library, the Og Mandino Conference Room, and the Stephen Covey Training Facility. I've learned from all of these greats—some of whom I've been fortunate to call friends, others of whom have mentored me in different ways. I plan to keep learning, improving, and developing until the day I die. I wholeheartedly agree with Albert Einstein, who said, "Intellectual growth should commence at birth and cease only at death."

> *An investment in knowledge pays the best interest.*
> —BENJAMIN FRANKLIN

The world is our oyster, and the way I see it, we're morally and ethically obliged to learn all we can and not waste our time (or at least not all of our time) looking at cat videos on the Internet!

Learning doesn't begin at birth and stop after you graduate

from school. It's a process that continues throughout your lifetime. We can never know everything—no one can. But what we *can* do is work hard to constantly improve ourselves—both professionally and personally—by always looking for ways to grow and maximize our potential. After all, improvement begins with "I."

THE SERGEY BRIN STORY

An Openness to Learn

There are people who come to this country who want to stay embedded in their own culture, their own language, and their own people. Now, this is understandable to a point—we all like to surround ourselves with the familiar and do what we can to preserve our heritage. But if you don't acclimate to your new surroundings and way of life, you'll never get beyond the lack of opportunity you left in your previous country. You won't ever become the success story you've dreamed about. Immigrants who make it big here are those who understand this and grasp the opportunity to grow. They have a drive to *learn*. The Russian immigrant Sergey Brin is a perfect example of this.

Everyone knows and uses Google, but few people know the story of its cofounder, Sergey Brin. In 1979, he and his family came to America from Moscow to escape persecution because of their Jewish faith. Brin certainly didn't rest on his laurels when he came here—he was *hongry*. He won a scholarship to the University of Maryland and, after receiving a degree in math and computer science, went on to study at Stanford University. There he met fellow student Larry Page, and the rest is history!

These two remarkable young men worked together on a research project. They didn't just talk about what they wanted to achieve—they *took action* to create a search engine that would list results according to the popularity of the pages. They called this search engine Google after the math term *googol*. Can you imagine how much hard work and dedication it took to get this mammoth project off the ground? I imagine they wanted to give up many times. I'm also sure they knew that nothing worthwhile ever comes easy. After much blood, sweat, and tears, and with investment from family, friends, and others, they launched the company in 1998 . . . and a phenomenon was born.

Google is now the most popular search engine in the world. As of April 2017, Google receives an average of 3.5 billion searches a day. Its founders are billionaires. But they are still working to get better, keep ahead of competitors, and offer the market new innovations. Undoubtedly, like the rest of us, they have faced their own challenges. Maybe they had to improve their judgment or discipline along the way. But by striving to *constantly improve*, they have become incredibly valuable to the marketplace and have helped make this country a leader in technology.

By the way, it's not just the technology sector that has benefited from successful immigrants. America has assimilated talented people from all over the world into its culture and economy, a fact that has made this country the leading global destination for research in many different fields. Did you know, for example, that in 2016 all six American winners of the Nobel Prize in the economics and scientific fields were immigrants? And that isn't a one-off. Stuart Anderson of the National Foundation for American Policy analyzed data on past Nobel winners and found that, since 2000, immigrants have been awarded 40 percent, or thirty-one of seventy-eight, of the Nobel Prizes won by Americans in chemistry, medicine, and physics. The countries of origin of the Nobel-winning immigrants include Japan, Canada, Turkey, Austria, China, Israel, South Africa, and Germany.

> *I want to be looked back on as being very innovative, very trusted and ethical, and ultimately making a big difference in the world.*
>
> —SERGEY BRIN

America is unique in this way. This country offers you a ladder to climb. You can start at the bottom, but by learning, growing, changing, and working hard you can climb all the way to the top.

CHAPTER TWELVE

Trait Two:

A Do-Whatever-It-Takes Mind-Set

What is a do-whatever-it-takes mind-set? Some people have negative connotations when they hear this expression. It can conjure images of ruthless egomaniacs who are determined to get their own way at all costs and disregard the opinions or feelings of others along the way.

To my mind, however, doing whatever it takes has a totally different meaning. Life favors the persistent and the willing. It's not just about doing your best—it's about having a certain attitude that enables that critical push to success. Those who make it in this world are those who get creative when they encounter roadblocks.

Successful immigrants are willing to get out of their comfort zones, do things they don't necessarily want to do, take risks, and make difficult decisions. They have passion and commitment, and they work tirelessly toward their goals. They learn from their mistakes, and they persevere through the dark times. This is the mindset that sets them apart.

So how can people who are born here do the same?

I once read a fable about a young man who desperately wanted to be successful. He heard of a guru who might be able to help him.

> *Energy and persistence*
> *conquer all things.*
> —BENJAMIN FRANKLIN

This guru lived on a mountaintop in a remote region, so the young man spent many days and nights traveling to meet him in the hope that the guru could tell him the secret to success. He endured many hardships and challenges along the way, traversing through dense forests, fighting off dangerous lions and bears, and surviving on very little food. At last, he got to the top of the mountain, where the guru sat silently meditating.

He fell to his knees. "Master," he pleaded, "teach me what I must do to succeed."

The guru said nothing. Instead, he got to his feet and beckoned for the young man to follow him. They walked back down the mountain, in silence, until they came to a lake. The guru gestured for him to kneel by the water's edge. He obliged. Suddenly, the guru grabbed him by the neck and forced his head under the water.

After a few seconds, the young man's lungs began to burn. *This is a test,* he thought to himself. *I must stay still.*

But more time passed and the guru still did not release his grip. The young man started to panic. He began to struggle and thrash around. He was going to drown! He twisted and turned, trying to free himself from the guru's hold, but he couldn't do it. Just as he felt sure he would die, the guru let him go and he came gasping to the surface.

"Young man," the guru said. "When you want success as much as you just wanted to breathe, that is when you will get it."

The fable's lesson is crystal clear. To succeed, you must want it with every fiber of your being—because only then will you do whatever it takes to get there.

A do-whatever-it-takes mind-set requires three things:

1. A KEEN PERSPECTIVE AND REMEMBRANCE OF WHERE YOU STARTED

There is a Haitian proverb that says, "Beyond the mountains . . . there are more mountains." It's ironic but true that very often when you have scaled your own particular mountain—financial, personal, spiritual—you get to the top only to see even more mountains ahead of you. It could be very easy to get discouraged by this, but instead of looking only at the new challenges ahead, remember to look over your shoulder to see how far you have come. Celebrate that the start line is now a long way off. It's all about perspective!

Remembering where you started is absolutely key for not giving up—for persevering to get where you want to go. Successful immigrants don't want to go back to where they began—that place of lack—so they don't allow themselves to forget what life was like before. It's important for them to remain humble and to remember their roots, and it's vital for them to constantly recall how far they have come and the hard work it took to get them where they are today. When you remember where you started, you will be motivated to keep moving forward—and to be grateful for how much you have achieved along the way.

2. A NEVER-SAY-DIE ATTITUDE

Having a never-say-die attitude means having a steely determination never to give up, no matter the odds or difficulties stacked against you. In my lifetime, I have heard many incredible stories about people with this attitude who have managed to overcome seemingly insurmountable challenges and achieve success as a result. Let me share two with you.

One of my favorite stories is about the design and construction of the Brooklyn Bridge in New York. The concept for the bridge was devised by an innovative German engineer and immigrant named John Augustus Roebling. Roebling was widely ridiculed for his dream of connecting New York City with Long Island—in fact, most people said the idea was so stupid that the entire bridge would end up in the East River!

> *A river cuts through rock, not because of its power, but because of its persistence.*
> —UNKNOWN

But Roebling never gave up his hope of achieving the impossible. Determined to succeed, he persuaded his son Washington to help him, and together they developed a workable model using innovative methods and materials. They began building in 1869, but, unfortunately, during initial works, Roebling was killed. Washington took over until, tragically, he was injured and left deaf, mute, and partially blind. Determined to carry on his father's dream despite his own life-limiting disabilities, he found a way to converse with his wife, Emily, about his construction and design plans, and she heroically took the lead on the project. In the end, the bridge took fourteen years to complete, and when it was finally finished, it was hailed as a modern miracle. Today, the Brooklyn Bridge stands as a stunning symbol of how sheer persistence made the seemingly impossible a reality.

My second story is just as inspiring, but in a different way.

When Babe Ruth said, "You just can't beat the person who never gives up," he could have been talking about British athlete Derek Redmond. Redmond's 400-meter race at the 1992 Barcelona Olympics is one of the most legendary Olympic stories ever. Redmond had devoted himself heart and soul to compete that year. Four years earlier, he had been unable to race in Seoul because of an Achilles injury and had a DNS—Did Not Start—next to his name. He vowed that this would never happen to him again, so he endured eight operations in four years to make it to the next Olympics.

In Barcelona, things started well. He had his sights on a medal and qualified for the semifinals by clocking the fastest time in his heat. On race day he charged out of the blocks, hitting his stride at the 250-meter mark. Suddenly, out of nowhere, he tore his hamstring. But incredibly, he ran on, refusing to give up. He decided he was going to finish the race if it was the last race he ever ran. He wasn't going to have a DNF—Did Not Finish—next to his name!

> *Ambition is the path to success. Persistence is the vehicle you arrive in.*
> —BILL BRADLEY

His father ran out onto the track to assist him, and with his support, Derek limped across the line. The crowd of 65,000 was on their feet, giving him a standing ovation, willing him to finish. It was the end of Derek's running career but certainly not the end of his influence. The footage has since been used by Visa, Nike, and the International Olympic Committee and has inspired millions of people all over the world.

So what did the heroes of these stories have in common? A determination never to give in or give up, no matter what. This never-say-die attitude is a hallmark of the successful immigrant.

3. A BELIEF THAT THERE'S NO SUCH THING AS FAILURE

The world of science is fascinated with failure and how humans react to it. In one study (outlined in *Mindset: How You Can Fulfill Your Potential*), researcher Dr. Carol S. Dweck set up a series of experiments to see how schoolkids between the ages of four and ten coped with challenge and difficulty. The first set of puzzles she gave the children was easy, but then they began to get progressively harder. Interestingly, the children's reactions to the increased difficulty were vastly different.

Some reacted positively. They liked the challenge and enjoyed learning new information. They believed that their abilities could be developed because they had what's called a "growth mind-set." They became deeply engaged with each task, processed the errors they made, learned from them, and then worked to correct their mistakes. But other students didn't cope as well. They perceived their failures as tragic, even catastrophic. Due to their more fixed-mind-set perspective, they felt judged by their lack of ability, and instead of believing they could complete the puzzles if they kept trying, they were devastated and, in turn, defeated.

Isn't it amazing that, even at such a young age, children could let their perception of failure influence them in a way that could affect them for the rest of their lives? Instead of simply thinking, *I haven't mastered this yet, but I will keep trying until I do,* they believed that they had failed at some core level and there was nothing they could do about it.

The truth is, if we want to grow, we shouldn't run from failure—we should engage with it and learn from it. Failing is not the end of anything. Sometimes, it's the beginning. Darren Hardy—motivational speaker, former publisher of *Success* magazine, and *New York Times* bestselling author—counsels that if you want to go far, you should fail fast and fail hard. He advises that you should embrace failure as a natural part of the success process. The idea is to get it over with quickly so that you see it's nothing to be scared of. Failure can only stop you if you let it.

Really, failure can be of enormous benefit. As an example, take Thomas Edison, one of the most successful and famous inventors in American history. His story is a virtual master class on the benefits of failure. Everyone can name the man who invented the lightbulb, but what's less known is that Edison worked on many inventions that were not successful, such as the electric pen and the electrographic vote recorder. What set him apart, though, was

> *I have not failed 10,000 times—I've successfully found 10,000 ways that will not work.*
> —THOMAS EDISON

his attitude concerning these so-called failures—he believed that just because something doesn't do what you planned for it to do, it doesn't mean the results are useless. In fact, he was of the opinion that negative results were just as powerful as positive ones, because you can never pinpoint what works the best until you can see what it does at its worst. For him, the most important part of the inventing exercise was not giving up. As he said, "Our greatest weakness lies in giving up. The most certain way to succeed is always to try just one more time."

Steven Spielberg was turned away from the University of Southern California three times before he became one of the most famous directors of all time. Oprah Winfrey was told she was unfit for TV. Failing at something or having a door closed in your face doesn't mean you will never get to where you feel destined to go. It just means that you haven't gotten there *yet*. Believing in "yet" is the mind-set of a successful immigrant. Really, failure is a vital part of success. If you don't fail, then you'll never fully know how to succeed.

THE ESTÉE LAUDER STORY

A Do-Whatever-It-Takes Mind-Set

One woman who certainly had a do-whatever-it-takes mind-set was the legendary Estée Lauder. Born in New York City in the early twentieth century to immigrant parents, Estée Lauder was raised above her father's small hardware store. Shortly after World War I began, her uncle, a chemist, came to live with the family. In a makeshift laboratory behind the house, he began to produce specialized skincare creams, with his young niece at his side. An entrepreneur at heart, Estée began selling these creams to her classmates—giving makeovers to prove their quality. Even at a young age, she recognized the importance of marketing and merchandising, saying, "To sell a cream, you sold a dream."

As she grew up, Estée continued to refine and improve her uncle's creams, cooking up mixtures on her own kitchen stove. She never forgot *where she started*. She was so passionate about her products that she gave free demonstrations and makeovers in salons, hotels, the subway, and even in the street! Creativity was her calling card when it came to making the next sale. One of her high points was when the manager of the prestigious Galeries La-fayette store in Paris said no to her products. The story goes that she "accidentally" spilled her fa-mous Youth-Dew perfume and bath oil on the floor during a crowded demonstration. As the aromatic scent wafted through the air, customers began ask-ing where they could buy it. Of course, the manager capitulated and gave Estée her initial order!

Estée *never said die.* Even times of serious finan-cial challenges didn't stop her. For example, turned away by ad agencies because of the small size of the company's ac-count, she invested her entire advertis-ing budget in prod-uct samples. These were then distrib-uted through direct mail, charity give-aways, and as gifts with purchases. Her "free gift with purchase" tech-nique went on to become a standard industry prac-tice.

> *The three great essentials to achieve anything worthwhile are, first, hard work; second, stick-to-itiveness; third, common sense.*
>
> —THOMAS EDISON

Estée *didn't believe in failure.* She launched her own skincare brand in 1946, taking on cosmetics gi-ants like Revlon, Helena Rubinstein, and Elizabeth Arden . . . and winning. Talk about David taking on Goliath! She was, as she put it herself, "a woman with a mission and single-minded in the pursuit of my dream." A trailblazer and the wealthiest woman in America, she created a family dynasty that continues to this day. The company now owns twenty-five major brands and is sold in 150 countries. It just goes to show that a lot of self-belief, creativity, hard work, and a do-whatever-it-takes mind-set can help you accomplish more than you can imagine.

When you're *interested* in achieving something, you mostly do what's convenient. When you're *committed*, however, you do whatever it takes. As the Japanese motto goes, "Fall down seven times, get up eight." Remember: The key to being where few people are is to start doing what few people do.

CHAPTER THIRTEEN

Trait Three:

A Willingness to Outwork Others

A willingness to outwork others is a key trait of any successful person, and certainly of successful immigrants. Those who come to this country with little more than hope to their name know that to get what they want they must work harder and longer than anyone else. As Thomas Edison once said, "We often miss opportunity because it's dressed in overalls and looks like work."

As you know, I had next to nothing when I came here, but within three years of getting my real estate license, I was one of the top real estate agents in America. I was willing to outwork others. I went all in and put everything I had into building my business from scratch. Soon, this attitude spread to other areas of my life, including my relationships and my health.

Being all in means putting all of your available resources—time, energy, money, capacity—into an effort. It's about having an up-at-dawn, down-at-dusk siege mentality. It means working so hard you leave nothing undone. You put your whole self on the table and don't hold anything back. As Nelson Mandela said, "There's no passion to be found in playing small."

In order to have a willingness to outwork others, you must:

> *Productivity is never an accident. It is always the result of a commitment to excellence, intelligent planning, and focused effort.*
> —PAUL J. MEYER

1. HAVE ALL-IN ENERGY AND EFFORT

If you're familiar with poker or another betting card game, you're familiar with the phrase "all in." Being all in means being 100 percent committed to reaching your goal and being willing to outwork everyone else to get where you want to go. Beverly is the ultimate personification of this spirit of all-in dedication and hard work. Persistence is her middle name. As well as being a loving wife and devoted mother, she is a former member of the U.S. Olympic Volleyball Team that went to Seoul, Korea. (Yes, this Irish immigrant from humble means married well above his station!)

> *Genius is one percent inspiration and ninety-nine percent perspiration.*
> —THOMAS EDISON

Beverly is often asked how she got to represent her country at the very pinnacle of her profession. The answer is always the same: she just kept working at it. As an All-American at the University of Tennessee, she dreamed of one day making the national volleyball team. Even though she was very highly regarded in college, she did not receive an invitation to try out for the U.S. team. Undeterred, she went and coached at the U.S. military academy at West Point for a year and kept training. She then began writing letters to the Olympic selection committee, and she enlisted her coaches, trainers, assistant coaches—basically anyone who had ever seen her play—to do the same. Finally, the committee said they would let her come and try out—if only she would stop writing letters!

When she got there, she was met by sixty-four other women who were the best volleyball players in the United States. She presumed they would choose at least twelve women so that they would have six players to scrimmage against six other players. The first day, after six-hour workouts of running and jumping, they cut twenty women. The following day, they cut fifteen, and the day after that they cut ten more.

Then, with a group of at least twenty women in the room they announced they were not going to select twelve women . . . they were going to select only nine. At 5'8", Beverly is shorter than most volleyball players. Most of her teammates were 6'2", 6'3", and 6'4". But she's a great athlete and has a phenomenal attitude. Something must have resonated with those selection coaches because, when they read out the names, she was ninth on that list—the last name called.

Still, her coach wasn't sold on her. He said, "It's four years until the Olympics. We're going to be bringing in hundreds of girls to try to take your spot. You have a very, very small chance of being here by the time we go to Seoul."

Over the next four years, hundreds of women did try out for that team. But Beverly continued to work and strive toward her goal. In fact, she won the coach's award as the person who was most coachable and hardworking on the team. Eventually, she got to make that trip to Seoul and fulfill her life's dream. Through sheer grit and determination, she finally reached her goal.

I will never forget the day she was inducted into the University of Tennessee Hall of Fame. There were more than 100,000 people at Neyland Stadium in Tennessee. Beverly—who was six months pregnant with our twins—was brought out into the middle of the football field and a 300-person band marched around her in the shape of the Olympic rings. Then they retired her number—a first for her alma mater. I remember standing there thinking, *How did I get so blessed and end up marrying this girl?* Again, thank God for the Emigrant Edge!

Over the next few pages, you'll hear Beverly's story in her own words. Beverly is a full-time mom and an educator, and she is always *all in to win*!

Growing up, I participated and competed in various sports on my junior high and high school teams. I played collegiate volleyball at the University of Alabama for two years and then transferred to the University of Tennessee. There, I was blessed to earn All-American and SEC MVP honors, respectively. I also coached the men's and women's volleyball teams at the United States Military Academy in West Point. The mission of West Point is to educate, train, and inspire the Corps of Cadets to become leaders who are committed to the values of duty, honor, and country, and who are ready for a career of professional excellence and service to the nation as United States Army officers. Coaching the cadets and witnessing their journey toward excellence encouraged me to achieve and propelled me to excel. My experience there definitely elevated my own game and proved to be a significant factor in shaping my philosophy on winning. It was the best mental training ground for the biggest challenge of my athletic career—training for the national team tryouts and making the cut for the USA Women's National Volleyball Team.

Now, I'm so proud to say I'm a former member of that team. We traveled the world competing against other nations, and we had a mantra from day one to "Win the Gold in Seoul" at the 1988 Olympic Games. We learned invaluable lessons along the way—some agonizing, many costly, and others glorious.

Although I've experienced a variety of coaching styles during my athletic career, there was always one theme they had in common: a confident belief that every athlete would give 100 percent for a winning effort every time he or she stepped out on the court or field.

This 100 percent commitment, or all-in mantra, has helped countless numbers of individuals and athletic teams to achieve great success in sports and in life. I've since incorporated this simple but profound coaching philosophy into all areas of my life. When you can't see light at the end of the tunnel, feel defeated, or are struggling with nagging problems that steal your energy, this mantra can move mountains, inspire you to make the necessary changes to overcome obstacles, and enable you to win!

All in to win . . . on being a godly woman: Like most of

you, one of my biggest challenges is balancing my time: getting enough rest, preparing healthy meals, taking care of the family, etc. Due to the many demands on my time, sometimes I can get overwhelmed and frustrated. However, because of my faith in God and my all-in commitment to being a godly example for our kids, I have learned to see these situations as trials—trials to test my patience and allow me to weather the toughest days.

All in to win . . . on being a mother: Motherhood is a huge responsibility and an enormous task. It's a profession of great sacrifice and service. There isn't anything easy about being a good mother. One woman said, "It can be back-breaking, heart-wrenching, and anxiety-producing—and that's just the morning!" I often focus on the problems and forget about celebrating the many joys of motherhood and the six, now seven (including Nicole, my daughter-in-law) wonderful blessings in our family. It's easy to grow weary with the many demands and challenges, but fortunately, I gather the courage to persevere and mother with passion through my faith in God. Being a mother is an area where I'm all-in through the good, the bad, and the ugly. Less than 100 percent commitment is not an option.

All in to win . . . on being a support for Brian: Supporting Brian in his endeavors has been an exciting journey. He promised me when we married that I'd never experience a dull day with him, and he was correct! It's been a journey filled with tremendous highs and some definite lows, but through them all, I can say that all of the ups and downs have served as stepping-stones for where we are today. The most important way I support Brian is through encouragement and by giving him ample space and time to achieve his goals. He is passionate about helping improve the lives of others. Every year, thousands are inspired by the content presented at his events. Months before an event, I watch him pore over videos and music, as well as research literature over and over again to prepare. He is passionately all in to win. I've learned from him that success isn't in the presentation, but in the preparation.

So what about you? Are you all in? Are you giving the absolute best you can with what you have? Are there areas in your life where you have lost your passion? If so, it's time to fan the flames and get back on track. Like my many coaches have taught me, I hope you give nothing less than 100 percent. If something's important to you, it's worth your very best. Analyze and evaluate all that's vital to you. Shake the negative talk, the negative people, and the past mistakes and failures. Enjoy the many highs, but be prepared to handle the low points and persevere through them. Napoleon said, "The greatest attribute of a soldier is not loyalty, it's not courage, it's endurance." If you need to push the restart button, go ahead. It begins with your all-in decision.

2. UNDERSTAND THE LAW OF THE HARVEST

We all know about the Law of Gravity—what goes up must come down—and the Law of Attraction—a focus on the positive attracts positivity in return. But what does the Law of the Harvest mean? It means that you reap what you sow, or to put it another way, what goes around comes around. Some people call it providence, others call it karma. I call it the keys to the good life!

In Ireland, farming and agriculture are the backbone of our national heritage. Farmers are experts when it comes to the Law of the Harvest. To ensure success, a farmer must water and fertilize the ground carefully, sow plentifully in the right season, and then watch over the crops diligently, guarding against pestilence and disease to ensure nurturing growth. If this is not done properly, all of the crops can be lost. There's nothing unplanned or spontaneous about farming—it's scheduled down to the minutest detail so that the utmost consideration can be given to each task at hand, and in the correct sequence. It's only when farmers have dedicated much time, energy, and careful attention to their endeavors that they can hope to reap the rewards of all that effort and labor. If only the same could be said of many people today! In this fast-paced, dog-eat-dog world, people want that profitable harvest, but they don't want to dedicate the time and care it requires to get it. They expect results fast, but they don't do the necessary groundwork. They're impatient and haphazard—and expect instant gratification. A farmer would shake his head in disbelief at this sort of approach. He would never expect the land to yield a golden harvest on demand—he knows he must put in the preparation and work first. He gives his all before he ever receives—he steps out in faith with hope and confident expectation.

Successful immigrants know that if you sow sparingly, you can't reap plentifully. You've got to put a lot of seeds in the ground and wait for a long period of time to be successful. And *waiting* isn't a passive term—you have to fertilize, water, and nurture before you can expect a harvest. In our world today, people want the harvest but they don't even want to drop seeds. Give and receive, reap what you sow—that's the Law of the Harvest.

3. HAVE A SENSE OF URGENCY

Many people like to dream of what they will be "someday." Unfortunately, for many, that someday never comes because it's nothing more than a pipe dream—a vague destination at a far-off point in the future. They forget that time and tide wait for no man and that, if you're not careful, "one of these days" often becomes "none of these days!" As Pablo Picasso once said, "Only put off until tomorrow what you are willing to die having left undone."

Successful immigrants don't sit around dreaming of someday, they get busy today making that dream come true. They have a sense of urgency. They aren't ruthless in their endeavors, but they are driven and focused. They don't just sit back and expect luck to happen—they make their own results by putting in all-in effort and energy and working like no one else. It's a funny thing, but I have always found that the harder you work, the better your results will be!

Now, this doesn't mean that you can never pause to take stock of where you're going. Everyone has to stop and catch their breath once in a while. In fact, it would be foolish not to. Here at Buffini & Company, our teachings are based on five elements: spiritual, relational, vocational, fiscal, and personal. The fact of the matter is it's not possible to be all-in in multiple areas of life simultaneously. Life has different seasons. Growth and development don't happen in every area all at once. One area of our lives may develop in one season, another area in a different season. The key is to remember that the balance we all want in our lives isn't really a state—it's about making small, almost imperceptible movements that help keep you balanced. It's like when you use the bosu ball in your gym. To stay balanced, you keep in motion.

Successful people don't let excuses override their drive. They know that their future is dependent on today's efforts, so even when they meet difficulty, they do not stop working toward their goal. They are relentless and dogged in their pursuit and never put off until tomorrow what they could do today. They don't just have good intentions—they are intentional in their approach to life and business. They understand that procrastination is the thief of time, so they do today what will help them tomorrow. Ask yourself, Is what I'm doing today getting me closer to where I want to be? Remember: When there's a hill to climb, waiting to start the ascent won't make it any less steep!

> *Begin to weave and God*
> *will give you the thread.*
> —GERMAN PROVERB

THE MADELEINE ALBRIGHT STORY

A Willingness to Outwork Others

M ost of us know Madeleine Albright as the first female U.S. Secretary of State. But how did she get to such a high position? Well, before she ever came to public prominence, she spent many years *outworking others* to achieve what she wanted.

The daughter of Czech diplomat Josef Korbel, she and her family fled to England after the Nazis occupied Czechoslovakia in 1939. Madeleine was just two years old. They ended up living in the part of London that was bombed the most during the war, but fortunately they managed to survive. For many years while growing up, she believed they had left her home country for political reasons, but she later learned that her family was Jewish and that three of her grandparents had died in Nazi concentration camps. The family returned home after the war ended but then fled to America in 1948 after the Communists seized power in Prague.

In America, Albright pursued education with a passion, giving it her *all-in energy and effort.* She graduated from Wellesley College in 1959 and later earned a master's degree from Columbia University. She went on to work as a fund-raiser for Maine senator Edmund Muskie and served as his chief legislative assistant. By 1976, she had received a PhD from Columbia and served on the National Security Council in the administration of President Jimmy Carter. During the Republican presidencies of Ronald Reagan and George H. W. Bush, she worked for several nonprofit organizations and taught at Georgetown University's School of Foreign Service as professor of international affairs. Really, she was sowing seeds for what was to come—she was *abiding by the Law of the Harvest.*

After Bill Clinton was elected president in 1992, Albright became ambassador to the United Nations. She quickly earned a reputation as a straight-talking defender of American interests, advocating for America's increased role in UN operations and demonstrating a *keen sense of urgency* about the work that needed to be accomplished.

> *All growth depends upon activity. There is no development physically or intellectually without effort.*
>
> —CALVIN COOLIDGE

In late 1996, Clinton nominated Albright to become U.S. Secretary of State—the first woman to hold that post. Her nomination was unanimously confirmed by the Senate, and she was sworn in on January 23, 1997. Her term ended when George W. Bush became

President in 2000. Though there was talk of her entering Czech politics, she returned to her teaching post at Georgetown and became chair of a nonprofit organization, the National Democratic Institute for International Affairs. Imagine all that this remarkable woman has achieved in her lifetime—and is still achieving. And it is all because of her willingness to work hard—and outwork others.

CHAPTER FOURTEEN

Trait Four:

A Heartfelt Spirit of Gratitude

I once overheard someone say, "Wherever you go, you can always find something to complain about." This remark struck a chord with me because there's so much truth to it! I have traveled all over the world and, believe me when I tell you, there has been plenty to complain about in almost every hotel in every country I have ever stayed. In some hotels the pillows are too hard, in others the bathroom is too small. Some places serve terrible breakfasts, others are too hot and stuffy. The list could go on and on.

Now, if I actually allowed myself to do all the complaining I could do, I would drive myself (and anyone who had the misfortune to travel with me) crazy! After all, these minor irritations are nothing more than first-world problems. How selfish and entitled would I be if I carried on this way?

And yet it's so easy to be sucked into this sort of negativity, isn't it?

We expect everything to be perfect all the time and become so impatient and get so aggravated when it's not. That's why expressing gratitude is so vital to a happy, fulfilled, and well-lived life. If we don't have gratitude in our hearts, we can easily become bitter and angry by what are nothing more than trivialities. Not only should we be grateful for the large and small everyday blessings in our lives, we should also be grateful for the setbacks because we learn the most from these.

The truth is, everyone encounters difficulties. Roses have thorns. Acorns must die in order for oak trees to grow. But from setbacks comes growth. If we took the time to make a list of all that we were thankful for in every aspect of our lives, I can guarantee it would take days, not hours.

For the past twenty years, I've had the privilege of teaching and training more than three million people in thirty-seven countries the strategies for attaining a good and prosperous life. I've met countless people who have shared their stories of transformation and triumph. Some of these were immigrants who had little financially but still expressed nothing but gratitude. Despite hardships and adversity, they believed themselves to be blessed! They were thankful for what others considered basic necessities, such as having somewhere safe and warm to lay their head at night or a job to go to every morning.

You will never hear these people moaning because their Wi-Fi is too slow or their latte isn't hot enough. They are too busy concentrating on what they do have. This tremendous heartfelt spirit of gratitude colors everything they do and how they view the world. Instead of seeing the negatives everywhere, they see all that is good and possible. If we all had this mind-set, imagine how much more positive and fulfilling our lives would be. Having a heartfelt spirit of gratitude is the most important trait of the successful immigrant—it's one we should all strive to imitate.

To have this attitude, you must:

1. KNOW THAT CICERO'S STILL RIGHT

For the past twenty-five years, our family has lived in San Diego county. But our home-away-from-home has been on the Big Island of Hawaii. Two things have always happened to us on every flight there: 1) The minute we get on the plane we start to relax and begin what we call our "Polynesian Paralysis." 2) At some point, one of the flight attendants will say to us, "Your children are amazing. They're so polite. We just don't see that anymore."

> *Gratitude is not only the greatest of virtues, but the parent of all others.*
> —CICERO

It's always great to hear feedback affirming our kids' conduct—every parent wants reassurance that they're doing a good job. But it's also disappointing to hear how rare gratitude and good manners are. We're not perfect parents, and we're not a perfect family; but if there's one thing we have done right, it's to instill and reinforce the importance of expressing gratitude. My children have grown up in a 10,000-square-foot home and have had many of the perks and benefits that come with economic success. But no one who meets them would think they are from a privileged background—gratitude is what others experience when they encounter our kids.

The flight attendants' remarks always encourage us that this focus on gratitude works. As every parent knows, reinforcing good manners or habits into our kids can seem like a never-ending task. But it is so worth the effort because an attitude of gratitude in our children can permeate every aspect of their lives—for their whole lives. Gratitude does more than just garner nice compliments from flight attendants or waitstaff; it becomes a foundation for how a person sees life for the better.

If you focus on what you're thankful for, you tend to concentrate on how much you have versus what you don't. You're more likely to compliment than complain. Petty molehills don't become mountains, and small irritations don't build up and damage or destroy valuable relationships. And if you're always filled with gratitude, you can never develop an arrogant attitude—it's impossible to have gratitude and entitlement at the same time!

I grew up in a small house in Dublin, with six kids (five boys, one girl) and my parents all squeezed into 720 square feet. The five of us boys shared a nine-by-nine-foot bedroom, and there was just one bathroom for all of us—there was a lot of squabbling in the mornings!

There was no heat in the home, but there was a lot of love, and our parents instilled in us an attitude of gratitude that is reflected in all of our adult lives today.

I can still hear my mother's voice saying, "It costs nothing to say 'please' or 'thank you.'" By drumming this into us, she was reminding us that if you don't commit to focusing on all you have to be grateful for and expressing gratitude on a daily basis, it's easy to lose perspective. The key to showing gratitude so you make the biggest impact is to do it by verbal or written expression.

I built a fortune in real estate, and I believe one of the most important reasons is because I sent my clients thank-you notes. I built my next fortune teaching business professionals the benefits of expressing gratitude, and today Buffini & Company provides more than ten million thank-you notes a year to those we train in the sales and service industries. That's right . . . showing gratitude will grow your business in a big way. But, better than that, it's a great way to live and the foundation for a good life.

In Japanese, there is a term, *on*. It means a sense of gratitude combined with a desire to repay others for what we have been given through words and deeds. Being grateful but not expressing it is pointless. Gratitude not expressed is ingratitude!

2. BE GRATEFUL TO THE CORE

For the past fifteen years, I've had the incredible fortune to fly on my own private plane. It's been a godsend for me because I've averaged being home with my family fifty-four more days every year than I would have without it. That's a lot of ball games I got to attend and family life experiences I didn't miss out on. Every time I board my plane, it still feels like the first time I ever set foot on it, and I can't believe that a guy like me, who started from such humble beginnings, gets to enjoy this experience. I'm so thankful.

One day, however, I was reminded just how easy it is to lose perspective. I was on a flight from New York to San Diego with some team members. We always have excellent food on the plane for our team, and we get to stay in nice hotels when we travel to our events. We'd already eaten a delicious meal in the early part of the flight when we stopped halfway to refuel. At this point, my typical practice was to have cheese, crackers, and a fruit plate for the second leg of the journey. Well, on this one occasion, we landed in Colorado Springs to refuel, and our pilot realized he had forgotten to order the usual midflight refreshments. One staff member, who traveled with me everywhere I went and who also came from humble means, proceeded to throw a temper tantrum.

I watched in disbelief as he pitched a fit about not having cheese and crackers, making the pilot feel worse than he already did. I thought to myself, *I've let this guy down*. He had lost perspective. We were on a private plane, traveling in luxury, and he was complaining that there were no crackers. It was surreal and deeply disappointing.

It was some years later that his superior came to me and said, "We can't deal with this guy's negativity anymore—he's got to go." Don't get me wrong, this man didn't lose his job because of cheese and crackers. But what I saw that day was only the tip of the iceberg in how far he had drifted from gratitude.

Being grateful is all about maintaining perspective. We stand in line in the fast-food restaurant thinking our food isn't fast enough, instead of remembering that countless people around the globe are going to bed hungry and would wait all day for less than what we are about to eat. We complain if our business isn't going as well as we would like, but we forget that there are places in this world where it's not even legal to have a business. Perspective is everything.

Our family's favorite holiday is Thanksgiving—a holiday based on gratitude. But for some, it's become more of a "turkey day" followed by binge shopping. Search online for images of Black Friday, and you'll see pictures both comic and tragic as people wrestle on the ground and punch each other in the parking lot to get a deal on a big-screen TV. It's ironic that such an attitude exists the very day after a holiday based on gratitude!

A number of years ago, we started a tradition of handing out notepads and pens after our Thanksgiving meal to make a list of everything we were thankful for over the past year. This might sound corny to you, but you've just got to try it. We play soft, classical, or baroque music while we make our lists of what we are grateful for that year.

When the kids were younger, I noticed that whenever we did this exercise I was always the first one finished. I would write down stuff like "I'm thankful for freedom, opportunity, and health," but as we'd share our lists, the kids would describe the flowers outside or the hummingbirds at the window . . . things neither Bev nor I ever thought of. Sometimes, in embarrassment, I would amend my list to at least include nature!

I also noticed that, as the kids got older, they seemed to see fewer of these details—and therein lies the problem. Why is it that when we're young we have more of a built-in appreciation for those simple blessings that we seem to lose later in life? When I have personally lost sight of what I am thankful for, I find myself gravitating toward criticism and negativity. The sure antidote for this is to count my blessings. I think of those less fortunate than me and immediately that internal whiny voice goes silent and I feel gratitude.

3. MAKE GRATITUDE YOUR ATTITUDE OF THE HEART

The great Zig Ziglar used to say gratitude stands for "Great attitude!" Having a great attitude is more likely to get you the promotion than get you fired. It's more likely to help you make the sale than not. And it will definitely help you make a good, strong, and lasting impression on everyone you meet.

Gratitude is an *attitude of the heart;* it brings energy to the spirit and does wonders for communication between people. We live in a constant barrage of news and information that sensationalizes and dramatizes the negativity of life. Those who choose to be positive are often dismissed as shallow or as idealists. On the contrary, it takes a tremendous amount of depth and character to be positive in such a negative world, to find the good around you whatever your circumstances.

Bev and I have two Hawaiian rocking chairs in our bedroom, and we start every morning by sitting in those chairs and sharing a prayer of gratitude, no matter what's going on. When you take time every day to speak out loud what you're thankful for and acknowledge what you do have, an attitude of gratitude becomes a habit. The temptation to complain is eliminated and cynicism disappears. When you name what you're thankful for, it's like drinking a smoothie for the soul!

One of the most incredible stories of gratitude I have ever read is of a couple from Seattle who left their entire estate to the American government in their will. Peter Petrasek and his wife, Joan, left over $800,000 to the U.S. Treasury when they died. Why? Because they were immigrants who were so grateful for the opportunities that this country had given them that they wanted to give back. Peter had fled Nazi persecution in his native Czechoslovakia and Joan had emigrated from Ireland to America as a young woman. According to the attorney who handled the couple's donation after their deaths, they bequeathed the money to the government because they wanted to make a statement about how much it meant to them to be American citizens.

This story stopped me in my tracks when I first read it. What must this couple's thought pattern have been for them to decide to do something like that? There must have been so much joy, appreciation, gratitude, and heartfelt spirit in their lives every single day. Their story was worth a fortune in and of itself!

Gratitude is transformational. It has the power to change your thinking from scarcity to abundance—and the capacity to change your focus from eternal pessimism to all that's great and possible.

I'm from a country that's known for its hospitality. In our native Gaelic language, the most common way to say "thanks a lot" is *"go raibh mile maith agat,"* which roughly translates as *one thousand thank-yous.* It's a great sentiment. If you bring that gratitude and energy into your dealings with others, people take notice. Don't focus on the difficulties you encounter. Focus on the fact that you're in the game. You always have something to be thankful for. That truth never changes.

THE PIERRE OMIDYAR STORY

A Heartfelt Spirit of Gratitude

Pierre Omidyar was born in Paris to Iranian parents who had fled the oppressive regime of their home country. The family moved to Baltimore when his father began a medical residence at the Johns Hopkins University Medical Center. As a child, Pierre was always interested in computers and would cut physical education classes to play on the school's computers. Instead of giving him detention for doing this, however, his forward-thinking principal hired him to write a computer program to print catalog cards for the school library, paying him six dollars an hour. It was the start of an illustrious career that eventually led to his magnum opus: to found eBay!

The story goes that the seeds of the idea for eBay came about when Pierre met his wife-to-be, Pamela. An avid collector of Pez dispensers, Pamela allegedly complained that she was having trouble finding like-minded people online. Eager to help, Pierre added a small auction service on his personal Web page so that she could talk to, buy from, and sell to other collectors all over the country.

Whether this is a tall tale or true, the fact is that the site took off immediately as collectors of all sorts of items—from Beanie Babies to household goods—flocked online to meet others. Pierre began charging a few cents to list an item and then collected a small commission if it was sold. Very soon, the company had become a three-billion-dollar empire with more than two million subscribers, and Pierre Omidyar was the head of one of the most popular and profitable Web-based businesses ever created.

"The biggest clue was that so many checks were piling up at my door that I had to hire part-time help to open them all," he told the *New York Times.* "I thought people would simply use the service to buy and sell things. But what they really enjoyed was meeting people."

The company went public in 1998. On its first day of trading, it was $18 per share. Four months later, it passed the $300 mark and Pierre was an instant billionaire.

Billionaire or not, in his heart, Pierre Omidyar still has a spirit of gratitude. Since leaving the day-to-day running of the company, he and his wife have donated more than $1 billion to good causes and have earned a Carnegie Medal of Philanthropy Award for their efforts to help tackle human trafficking and health issues, as well as to embolden entrepreneurs.

"I created [eBay] with the belief that people are good. If you give people the opportunity to do the right thing, you'll rarely be disappointed," he told the *Huffington Post.* "After eBay became so financially successful, I really felt a sense of responsibility to put that to good use."

Why does he do all this good work? Because he wants to give something back and express his gratitude. What a way to do it!

CHAPTER FIFTEEN

Trait Five:

A Boldness to Invest

We all know what it can feel like when you have to make a decision and you just don't know what to do. When there are too many options to choose from, it can make you freeze and do . . . nothing. Some people behave like this their whole lives. They forever sit on the fence, paralyzed with fear, unsure of what direction to take and which way to jump.

Unfortunately, sitting on the fence gets you nowhere—it's just the perfect spot from which to watch life pass you by. People who succeed don't let paralysis take over when they need to make a choice about what to do. One way or another, they make a decision. Even though they might be nervous or unsure, they know they must take bold action.

Immigrants certainly can't afford to let life's many choices dazzle and confuse them. If they have a desire to succeed, they have to be bold and focus on the outcome they want. That means investing in themselves, in their vocation, and in other people. The great immigrants don't just play with one chip or two; they put in everything they have. That's why they're able to grow businesses as well as economies. They can literally transform countries because of their desire to invest and grow. As Richard Branson said, "The brave may not live forever, but the cautious do not live at all."

Bold investments require that you:

1. INVEST IN YOURSELF

I love the movie *The Help,* which is based on the novel by Kathryn Stockett. One of my favorite scenes is when a maid teaches a little girl how to have more self-belief by getting her to repeat the mantra "You is kind, you is smart, you is important." Really, we should all look ourselves in the eye every day and say the same thing!

In today's tough world, it can take a lot to believe in yourself. We are constantly bombarded with messages that fill us with doubt about our ability. Are we good enough? Do we have enough? How does our success compare to other people's? Well, as the old saying goes, comparison is the thief of joy and the death knell of success. We should spend far less time comparing ourselves to other people and much more time working on our own goals. Successful immigrants know that coveting what others have doesn't help to achieve dreams.

So how do you combat self-doubt and not fall into the comparison trap? One way is to invest in yourself. Whether it's learning a new skill, improving yourself personally or professionally by taking a class, or even making the decision to hire a coach, it's important to work on yourself so you can reap rewards and, in turn, help other people.

Jim Rohn's top tip for success is to make yourself more valuable to the marketplace. He once said to me; "Brian, work harder on yourself than you do on your job. If you do, you'll go from making a living to making a fortune." This is one of the best pieces of advice I have ever been given, and taking it to heart has reaped immeasurable dividends.

So why don't more people invest in themselves? There are a number of reasons. Often, people believe they can't afford to—be it investing time, energy, or finances. They have so much else going on in their lives. They have bills to pay and obligations to meet—how can they afford to invest in themselves? My answer? They can't afford not to!

Another reason is that people sometimes almost subconsciously believe that they aren't worth investing in. They have an internal monologue constantly running in their heads telling them that any accomplishments thus far were due more to chance than actual talent. There's even a term for this thinking: *impostor syndrome*. First identified in the late 1970s by scientists Pauline R. Clance and Suzanne A. Imes, *impostor syndrome* is the belief that you don't deserve the success you have. Deep down, you think you're a fraud and, sooner or later, people are going to find out. According to a recent study in the *International Journal of Behavioral Science,* up to 70 percent of Millennials suffer from this condition.

Perhaps it's no wonder: With so many challenges and advances facing us every day, we can often feel forced to fake that we know what we're doing when, in reality, we don't. To the naked eye, we might look like swans gliding calmly across the lake, but underneath the water, we're paddling like crazy just to keep up. Surprisingly, Maya Angelou knew all about this syndrome. She once said, "I have written eleven books, but each time I think, 'Uh oh, they're going to find out now. I've run a game on everybody, and they're going to find me out.'" And I have discovered that I'm not immune either.

When I first came to America, I suffered from a case of *impostor syndrome* that I covered up by kidding around. I constantly joked about myself the way I always used to back home in Ireland. If anyone told me how well I was doing, I laughed off the praise. I was uncomfortable with it. And I certainly didn't want anyone to think I was getting too big for my boots! You see, we Irish are by far the most self-deprecating breed on this earth. In fact, I believe that talking ourselves down is a peculiarly Irish condition. We are especially gifted at it—if there were an Olympic medal going for this ability, we'd win it every year!

But one day a client challenged me about this habit. "Why do you rag on yourself all the time?" she asked.

I told her I was just kidding around.

"It's good not to take yourself too seriously, I guess," she mused. "Just make sure people know you take your *work* seriously."

Now that made me think! Was it possible that people thought I wasn't a hard worker? I was trying to be humble, brushing off compliments, but was I subconsciously giving people a message that I lacked confidence in myself or wasn't capable?

From that moment on, I decided to change how I spoke to myself. I took advice from Lou Tice, who said in his seminal work,

Smart Talk, that we either imprison ourselves or advance ourselves with our own thought processes. The key to what we need is in our heads—all we have to do is talk ourselves up for success. But this seems easier said than done.

The truth is, continually diminishing your accomplishments is a product of a lack of self-esteem. You should be able to live without others' accolades, of course, but you should be able to accept them too. After all, if you don't respect yourself enough to recognize your gifts and talents, how can you expect other people to respect you?

Many people dabble in the stock market, hoping to make good on their money. But investing in yourself will bring one of the best returns you could ever get. It not only sends a powerful message to your subconscious that you are worthwhile, it also sends a powerful message to people around you—they see that you recognize your own value and potential. It tells people that you believe in yourself and you're going to get great results by working on your potential. That's not arrogance; it's respect for yourself and your natural talents. Your talents are God's gifts to you—what you do with them is your gift to God.

Only by investing in yourself will you make the most of your abilities. Only by becoming the best version of yourself will you be able to serve others better. Treat yourself as you would treat a good friend. You wouldn't discourage, disrespect, or diminish a friend's attempts to be a better person, would you? So why do it to yourself? After all, if you don't invest in yourself, then who will?

Warren Buffett, one of the wealthiest people in America, is famous for his investing views and strategies. Through a shrewd investment strategy, he has led his company, Berkshire Hathaway, to incredible growth over the years. And yet he believes that the greatest investment you can ever make is in yourself.

In an ABC News interview in July of 2009, when asked whether it is still important for families to send their children to college or other forms of higher learning, Buffett said: "Generally speaking, *investing in yourself is the best thing you can do.* Anything that improves your own talents; nobody can tax it or take it away from you. They can run up huge deficits and the dollar can become worth far less. You can have all kinds of things happen. But if you've got talent yourself, and you've maximized your talent, you've got a tremendous asset that can return ten-fold."

I think we should take this sage advice from the "Oracle of Omaha." He knows a thing or two about making wise investments. After all, a $1,000 investment in Berkshire Hathaway in 1964 is worth approximately $10 million today!

2. INVEST IN YOUR VOCATION

According to Mr. Webster, a vocation is a strong desire to spend your life doing a certain kind of work. How many people today can say that their work is something they feel so passionately about that they are *compelled* to do it? I'm guessing it's a fortunate few! But it doesn't have to be this way.

Knowing yourself is the first step to knowing what your true vocation is. Watch for the clues that continually show up in your life. Your unique gifts and abilities begin from an early age. Think back on your life. What has been a recurring theme? What have you enjoyed doing? What are you good at? If you pay attention, then what engages and inspires you will soon become obvious.

We've all heard the old saying "Love what you do and you'll never work a day in your life." It's certainly true that if you love what you do then life becomes a whole lot more fulfilling! I consider myself very blessed in this way because I discovered at an early age where my passions lie. My light-bulb moment happened on a school trip to Rome, Italy, when I was a teenager.

> *Do you see a man skilled in his work? He will stand before kings.*
> —PROVERBS 22:29 NIV

One day, my classmates and I went on an excursion to an outdoor market and I saw a suede jacket that I really wanted to buy. There was only one little problem—it was way out of my price range. But that small detail wasn't going to stop me—I was determined to find a way to get it.

Over the following days, I went back to that market multiple times, observed the vendor dealing with his customers, and carefully watched how he did business. Eventually, we started talking and he confided that the tourists didn't know how to barter properly—they gave in far too quickly and easily. Suddenly, I knew what I had to do—I had to barter like a local. I went to another vendor, one who also had the jacket I wanted, and used my new-found information to bargain with him for it like my life depended on it. I haggled like a professional, loving every second of the deal-making. To my delight, my efforts worked! My friends were extremely impressed with my skills, even more so when our teacher arrived wearing exactly the same jacket for which he had paid far more. In fact, "robbed blind" would be the operative term for it!

When he heard my tale of triumph, his jaw dropped, and so did the jaw of our headmaster. He called me to one side. To be truthful, I was half afraid he was going to reprimand me for haggling on the street and somehow bringing the good name of our Irish Catholic school into disrepute in the Holy City. But it turned out he wanted a jacket too—and he wanted me to get it for him at the best possible price. My new skill set was suddenly in high demand! In the end, I not only got him a jacket at a great price, I helped many other teachers get a great deal that day. It was the most fun I'd ever had.

From then on, I realized that helping people and working in sales was for me. The buzz of making a deal and helping someone get what they wanted was unlike anything I'd ever experienced before—and I knew without a shadow of a doubt that I wanted to do it for the rest of my life.

Like I say, I consider myself very fortunate because I came to this realization early on. Many people reach middle age before they know what it is they want to do with their lives—and some people never discover their true calling. But I knew, from that moment, that helping people and impacting and improving their lives was my true vocation. Since then, it has been my life's work to invest in my vocation by fulfilling my calling to the very best of my ability.

Not only have I invested in myself by spending time on personal growth and stretching myself to reach my full potential, I have also invested in my vocation by studying as much as possible to become not only knowledgeable but an expert in my field.

Finding your true vocation is only the first step—you must then invest in it.

3. INVEST IN OTHERS

Community is the backbone of societies around the world. We're all interconnected and reliant on one another, be it for protection, support, help, or just the need to connect. We Irish, for example, do a pretty good job of connecting with others through music, story, and the occasional tip of a glass! Whether it's in neighborhoods, churches, societies, or whatever else, people just do better together, a fact that all successful immigrants know only too well. Yes, investing in other people pays great dividends . . . but only if you invest in the right people.

> *Alone we can do so little.*
> *Together we can do so much.*
> —HELEN KELLER

My mother used to say to me, "Show me your friends and I'll tell you who you are." In other words, who you associate with and invest in is very important. It's vital to have positive people in your life—friends, colleagues, mentors, coaches. You must surround yourself with people who will support and help you achieve your goals and dreams, not those who discourage or undermine you.

Throughout my life, I have invested in many people, just as they have invested in me. However, I have learned some difficult lessons along the way. I truly believe that as you become successful you must share that success with others. I always say, "Take someone in the carpool lane of success with you. But, before you do, you have to make sure that they really want it in their heart. They can't just say they want it—they must *demonstrate* they want it."

My mission is to impact and improve the lives of people. I travel the world fulfilling this mission. The systems I teach, the programs I encourage people to take, and the goals I have people set are then reinforced by a great team of coaches and trainers who help our individual clients achieve these goals. Buffini & Company has coached more than 100,000 people in a one-to-one capacity and has trained more than three million worldwide.

On an individual level, I also mentor people one-on-one. However, I've often found that I want their success more than they do. Typically, what happens is I have lunch or coffee with someone who says they want some input or help. I will usually recommend and then send that person a book to read. (More than 50 percent of my assistant's office space is dedicated to bookshelves. We give away more than 500 books a year to people who write to me, whether it's clients or people who listen to "The Brian Buffini Show" podcast.) The next time we meet, I'll ask that person how they liked the book I sent. If they say they haven't read it yet, I'll know they are not ready to achieve the success they say they want. I will not offer any more advice, give any more of my time, or spend any more energy on them until they read the book and take the next step.

The truth is, you can't want someone's success more then they want it for themselves. Investing in people is important, but you must invest only to the degree that they desire to achieve it themselves. Otherwise you're setting that person up for failure, and your relationship is ultimately going to become strained because you will become frustrated with their lack of progress.

The best investment I ever made in other people, besides my family, is the community of people at Buffini & Company. When we first began, we were a small band of individuals united with a common purpose: to impact and improve the lives of others. Today, our company in Carlsbad serves more than forty separate industries. Approximately 80 percent of our clients are in the real estate industry. And even though we coach fewer than 2 percent of all agents nationwide, our clients sell one in every eight homes in America. That's a lot of ripples in a lot of ponds!

In his book *Think and Grow Rich*, acclaimed author Napoleon Hill spoke of the power of the mastermind and that 1 plus 1 together made 11 when it came to the power of people. I have seen this evidenced time and time again in my business. We've seen our business continually develop over the past two decades because we have invested in our community of staff and customers.

Buffini & Company has recently been named as a "Top Workplace" by the *San Diego Union-Tribune*. We give our staff a great working environment, acknowledgment for a job well done, and compensation that rewards their efforts. They give our clients great service, personal attention, and the extra-mile mentality. In turn, our clients give us business and endorse our work to their sphere of influence and network. What goes around comes around!

Our business community is thriving. The people we coach and train are now a community who connect independently of us. Think about the significance of that. Most businesses have clients whom they've never even met, but our customers, who reside across North

America and work in multiple industries, actually host their own get-togethers and parties and are often involved in charities together. The bonds are incredibly profound. For example, when one of our clients was diagnosed with a terminal illness, our community of clients organized a fund-raiser to help with costs. And a number of years ago, following the disaster of Hurricane Katrina, we created a fund in partnership with Habitat for Humanity to build homes in Baton Rouge for displaced people. All we needed was the people. I was so proud and humbled when our clients showed up in droves and built houses together. It was a true testament to the importance of investing in others. That spirit of community never ceases to amaze me.

> *Individually, we are one drop. Together we are the ocean.*
> —RYUNOSUKE SATORO

THE NORDSTROM STORY

A Boldness to Invest

In 1887, a hardworking sixteen-year-old named John W. Nordstrom left his home in Sweden for America. He arrived with five dollars and not a word of English. The first years in the Land of Dreams were extremely difficult for him—he did hard labor in mines and logging camps and even traveled to Alaska in search of gold. Eventually, he settled in Seattle and set up business with Carl Wallin, a friend who owned a shoe-repair shop downtown. In 1901, John invested some of his gold earnings and he and Carl opened Wallin & Nordstrom, a small shoe store.

Nordstrom had a *boldness to invest*—he was bold enough to take a chance and go to Alaska, bold enough to bet on himself and dig in the dirt for years, and then bold enough to invest his earnings in a brand-new venture. This boldness of spirit translated into how he ran his new shoe store too. From the start, Nordstrom's approach to business was to provide exceptional service, selection, quality, and value. His motto was to do "whatever it took" to keep the customer happy. The word about his excellent customer service spread. The store grew a loyal customer base, and the company expanded quickly, thanks to a boldness to invest in his staff and his customers. Soon, from this humble shoe store, Nordstrom, Inc. and the world-famous Nordstrom way of taking care of customers was born.

Today, a fourth generation of the Nordstrom family is at the helm of the company. From one tiny shoe store, Nordstrom is now a retail giant with a global reach and is still the standard against which other companies measure themselves. The constant is John W. Nordstrom's founding philosophy: offer the customer the best possible service, selection, quality, and value. This philosophy reaps tremendous commercial rewards. In 2015, the company achieved an all-time-high for total net sales of $14.1 billion. But it's not all about the money: The company operates a give-back model, donating a percentage of all profits to charities.

CHAPTER SIXTEEN

Trait Six:

A Commitment to Delay Gratification

We live in a world of instant gratification. People aren't prepared to wait in line at a store, they get upset when a website takes longer than a few seconds to load, and they hang up the phone in frustration if they are put on hold. The world is now so fast-paced that almost everything is available at the flick of a switch: You can order a product online and get it delivered the same day; you can stream your movies directly to your device; you can share your photos instantly on . . . you guessed it, Instagram. These days, there's instant access or an app for everything!

Now, there's no denying that split-second access to just about everything is convenient, but it has many downsides too. The presumption of immediacy has become so ingrained in us that if something isn't instant, it's instantly discarded, and that's not healthy. Perhaps the biggest effect is on our kids, who have never had the opportunity to learn the value of waiting for anything. According to a recent study by the Pew Research Center (Internet & American Life Project), people under the age of thirty-five have hyperconnected lives with "negative effects [that] include a need for instant gratification and loss of patience."

My father always told me "patience is a virtue," but these days it seems no one has even an ounce left. People now prefer to play a quick game on their phone instead of taking the time to read a book or newspaper. Many have become consumers of shallow information, meaning their view of the world is skewed and often unrealistic. In an age where stories of kids creating multimillion-dollar apps in coffee shops abound, many people expect to achieve overnight fame and fortune by doing almost nothing!

The truth of the matter is that worthwhile accomplishments require time. Take saving, for example. In 2012, the U.S. Department of Commerce Bureau of Economic Analysis found that Americans' personal saving rates—the percentage of disposable income saved—averaged 3.6 percent. Thirty years earlier, in 1982, Americans saved 9.7 percent.* Now, there could be many reasons for this spectacular drop, from unemployment to poor wages, but it's very probable that society's growing focus on instant gratification has played a part. We're so caught up in the fast-paced immediacy of the here and now that we no longer think about end results. We're losing our ability to think long term and be satisfied.

Not everyone, however, has this mind-set. Successful immigrants *do* think long term. They are patient with growth. They don't need

---

* Bostonglobe.com.

instant gratification. They know that good things come to those who wait . . . and work.

Many people think that the rich are extravagant and like to show off their wealth, but the opposite is often true. Many of the wealthiest people I know are extremely low-key. They don't drive new cars. They don't live in mansions, own Rolexes, or drink champagne. Just because you're a millionaire doesn't mean you are flashy. Most millionaires live ordinary lives—but they have some extraordinary qualities. For example, in *The Millionaire Next Door*, Dr. Thomas J. Stanley and Dr. William D. Danko found that those who had a net worth of $1 million or more shared fundamental qualities that were opposite to today's instant gratification and consumption culture. These qualities included living below their means, ignoring conspicuous consumption, and choosing the right occupation.

I have to say, I have never expected crazy returns or to double my money in a short amount of time. I preferred to work for it and to chip away, little by little. I like to rely on my own judgment and faculties so much that I've never even bought a lottery ticket. Why? Because I would hate to win!

I've always wanted to grow my own success. I wanted to be part of the process, and I wanted it to be part of me. That's why, when I finally did achieve success, I embraced it with every cell in my body because I had earned it with very fiber of my being. When you sacrifice, you truly appreciate the reward. It means far more to you because it *hasn't* come easy. You have personally paid the price.

A commitment to delay gratification means that you:

1. CHOOSE THE "S" WORD—SACRIFICE

When you see a successful person, you usually only see the public triumphs and not the personal sacrifices they have made to get to where they are. You don't witness the painful reality of what it takes to succeed.

Over the years, I have made countless sacrifices. For example, because I travel a lot for work, I have missed many of my kids' sports games, recitals, birthday parties, and bedtimes. Likewise, I have missed date nights and anniversaries with my wife. We travel a lot now as a family, but when we were starting out, there were many years we didn't go on vacation because we just didn't have the money.

I remember the first time I went to visit Beverly's family down South; her grandfather took me out fishing. He was a man of few words, and I felt a little nervous around him. We sat in that boat, waiting for the fish to bite, mostly in silence. Eventually he said, "You fixing to marry my granddaughter, son?"

"Yes, sir," I stuttered.

"Well, romance without finance leads to the ambulance. Remember that."

I have never forgotten his words of wisdom!

Beverly is a patient woman who has stuck with me when times were lean . . . and believe me, they were lean. I remember one time I wanted to treat her to a special getaway but, of course, I couldn't afford it. Then I came across a newspaper ad for a resort in Palm Springs. The hotel and the facilities looked out of this world, and unbelievably, it was in my budget. I thought there must have been some sort of mistake, but when I called, the hotel confirmed it for me—they would give me an incredible deal for ninety-nine dollars a night. They would even upgrade us to a suite for the weekend! Well, I couldn't believe it and neither could Beverly when I told her I was taking her to a five-star hotel. When we got there, I understood why it was such a good value: Palm Springs is slap-bang in the middle of the desert . . . something this Irish immigrant hadn't even realized!

It was so hot we couldn't go outside. We couldn't sit by the pool or even go for a walk during the day. I could only play golf at night! But, you know, it was cheap, so for years we went to Palm Springs in August because we couldn't afford to go there any other time of the year.

Now, all joking aside, those years were quite tough. The truth is, it's challenging to budget. It's difficult not to spend when you've been working so hard. In this instant gratification age, it's tough to say no to store cards and easy credit. It's hard to make the decision to sacrifice in the short term to get what you want in the long term. For years, we watched every nickel, saving for our children's future or reinvesting back into the company. But the hardest part for me was never the financial sacrifices—it was missing out on precious time with my family. Fortunately, we are an extremely tight unit who always made sure to make up for time missed. For some people, the toll this kind of sacrifice takes can have cata-

> *If you do what is easy, your life will be hard, but if you do what is hard, your life will be easy.*
> —LES BROWN

strophic results—the trade-off is a broken home and fractured relationships.

2. KEEP YOUR EYES ON THE PRIZE

The greatest and most successful immigrants are focused. They keep their eyes on the prize, moving forward by taking small steps to reach their ultimate goal or destination. They manage their time in a deliberate way and don't get distracted by the false promise of fame or material goods. They focus on the end result, while also appreciating the journey. When your goal is top of mind, the path to it may be challenging, but it is also strewn with a wealth of learning and opportunity.

I have a friend, an immigrant from Russia, who has worked as a laborer ever since he arrived in this country. Like me, he came here with virtually nothing and now he's a millionaire. How did he do it? By keeping his eyes on the prize and being faithful to just one small thing.

This man used the money he earned from Monday to Friday to provide for his family and meet his obligations. He worked on Saturday too. But with that money he did something different—he invested every penny into property, systematically building his portfolio over the years, all the while living below his means. He was careful, methodical, and systematic in his approach. He wasn't in

> *I hated every minute of training, but I said, "Don't quit. Suffer now and live the rest of your life as a champion."*
> —MUHAMMAD ALI

it for a fast buck, he was in it for the long haul, and his patience and perseverance have paid off.

3. UNDERSTAND THE COMPOUND EFFECT

We all know the story of the tortoise and the hare. When the two animals set off on a race, the hare ran off ahead. Then, confident that he was certain to win, he stopped for a nap and fell into a deep sleep. Meanwhile, the tortoise moved slowly but steadily ahead, one small step at a time. In the end, it was the tortoise, not the hare, that won, because of his consistency in taking all those small, seemingly insignificant steps forward. Hence the expression: "Slow and steady wins the race."

In life, this mind-set is what sets successful people apart. Sure, speed can be great, but being blinded by speed to the detriment of real progress is a huge mistake. If you are consistent with the small things, like all successful immigrants, you will win. Small, smart choices made consistently pay huge rewards.

Darren Hardy illustrates this concept in *The Compound Effect*. In the book, he tells the story of three friends—Larry, Scott, and Brad—who grew up together. They all live in the same neighborhood and have similar lifestyles and salaries. Likewise, they all want something to change in their lives.

Larry plods along, doing what he always has, feeling vaguely discontented with how things are but not willing to do anything differently. Scott decides to makes some simple changes. He starts by reading ten pages of a good book every day and listening to thirty minutes of something instructional or inspirational on his commute to work. He also cuts 125 calories from his diet and begins to walk a couple of thousand extra steps every day. Meanwhile, Brad wants to have a little more fun in his life, so he buys a big-screen TV, takes up cooking, and adds one alcoholic drink to his evenings. Again, all small, seemingly inconsequential choices.

At the end of five months, there are no perceivable differences among the three friends. It's the same at the end of ten months. But, by about month twenty-five, measurable differences begin to appear. At month twenty-seven, there are significant differences and, by month thirty-one, the differences are incredible.

Everything is more or less the same for Larry, except he is even more discontent than before. Brad is now fat and very unhappy. Scott, on the other hand, is not only trim and fit, but because of the positive reading and listening habits he has made, he has been promoted and his marriage is better than ever.

Now, to someone on the outside looking in, the change in Scott's life could look like some kind of overnight miracle. But really what has happened is that the compound effect has kicked in. Scott isn't an overnight success; he has transformed himself by making small, smart, and consistent choices over a prolonged length of time.

This is the magic of the compound effect and it's what successful immigrants use to get ahead, slowly and steadily. They know that good habits, discipline, and hard work will produce success in time. They don't expect instant gratification, nor would they welcome it. They still respect the idea of paying their dues for success, like generations did before them. They haven't forgotten the importance of the qualities that our forefathers valued so much.

They know that there are no formulas or quick fixes for success. When Beverly was chosen to represent her country on the Olympic volleyball team, it wasn't because she got up that morning and got lucky. The harder she worked, the luckier she got. She did many thousands of hours of drills and practice. Long after others had given up, she refused to give in. She faced hardships and heartbreak along the way, but by keeping faithful to the small, daily practices, she enjoyed the compounding effect in the end. As Zig Ziglar once said, "Hurricanes and earthquakes get all of the publicity, but termites do more damage and they take such little bitty bites!" One tiny change can make all the difference whether you're trying to adopt new habits, manage your business more effectively, or keep your goals in sight. When you make a small change, it creates a ripple effect—you become motivated to make another small change and then another. When I interviewed Zig's son, Tom, for my podcast, we discussed the impact of making small changes. He broke it down for listeners, saying if you make a small change fifty-two times, or even twelve times, in a year, you'll have a new life. Big changes are tough to commit to, and when we're unable to keep it up, we feel as if we've failed. On the other hand, small changes are easy to make and when you do them consistently, you'll get a shot of motivation. Want to make a difference in your life today? Start small.

> *Compound interest is the eighth wonder of the world. He who understands it, earns it. He who doesn't, pays it.*
> —ALBERT EINSTEIN

THE MARSHMALLOW EXPERIMENT

A Commitment to Delay Gratification

I n the late 1960s and early 1970s, a series of studies on delayed gratification were held at Stanford University. During these experiments, researchers offered children a choice: one small reward—often a marshmallow—that they could eat immediately, or two small rewards—two marshmallows—if they waited about fifteen minutes before eating the first one. During these fifteen minutes, the researchers left the room and the child was alone. Of course, some kids ate the treat immediately, but others resisted temptation, delaying their gratification, and were rewarded with an extra treat.

The truly interesting part is that, in follow-up studies, researchers found that the children who were able to wait for the two marshmallows tended to have better outcomes in life. They fared better on SAT scores, their health was better (for example, their BMI was lower), and their parents reported that they were significantly more competent as adolescents.

So, does being unable to exert self-control as a child mean you are doomed to a life of failure? Of course not, but it does mean that being able to delay gratification is a reliable predictor of success. Delaying gratification may not come naturally, and it can certainly be stunted by society's 24/7 mind-set, but it's a key skill that can be learned no matter where you are in life.

Success isn't like instant coffee—you can't just add water and stir. You must first fertilize the soil, then nurture the coffee beans, and, finally, harvest in good time. Only then will you truly reap what you sow and enjoy the sweet taste of success!

> Never give up what you want most for what you want today.
>
> —NEAL A. MAXWELL

CHAPTER SEVENTEEN

Trait Seven:

An Appreciation of Where
They Came From

My parents still live in the house I grew up in. The Buffini "compound," as we like to call it, has three small bedrooms and one bathroom. There were eight of us crammed into that house during my childhood, ten on the weekends when our grandparents came to stay. But, despite these modest accommodations, we were very happy.

These days, I live in what most people would consider a mansion. I have all the luxuries that money can buy. But I make sure to always remind myself of my past and where I came from so that I remember to appreciate my present circumstances. I want an attitude of gratitude to guide me in how I live my life. I want to remember how far I've come. More important, I want to help others get to where they want to be. Remembering where I came from means that I focus on living my life as an example of what can be.

When I talk about my roots, most people are interested in how I came from little and achieved so much, but a few misunderstand my motives when I tell my story.

One day, a man approached me. Frowning, he said, "Would you stop saying that you started with ninety-two bucks in your wallet?"

I asked him why that bothered him and he replied, "Well, it's kind of self-aggrandizing."

I said I understood his viewpoint, but then I told him the truth about why I always talk about where I came from.

"I'm not saying these things in a boastful way," I replied. "I *need* to remember where I came from. I never want to forget it. And I believe it gives people hope, based on their circumstances."

Remembering where you came from gives you perspective, reminds you to be grateful, and keeps you humble. I have a painting by artist Edwin Hayes from the National Gallery of Ireland outside my office. It depicts an emigrant ship leaving Dublin Harbour in the 1850s. Each day I pass by that painting I'm reminded how far I have come in my life. And then I thank God for all that my predecessors did to help me get to this place and for all the opportunities this country has given me.

An appreciation of where you came from requires:

1. A GROUNDED IDENTITY

On February 19, 2002, exactly seventy-five years to the day that my grandfather had become an American citizen, I pledged my allegiance to the American flag. It was both one of the greatest and one of the hardest days of my life. I still vividly recall the great joy I felt as I drove home singing along to Ray Charles's "America the Beautiful!" I was so proud and happy. But I also remember the mixed emotions I experienced when I raised my right hand and swore allegiance to a flag that wasn't the one I grew up with. That was bittersweet.

I will never lose sight of the fact that this country has given me so many opportunities. From working in a Fotomat to selling T-shirts on the beach to working in real estate and then to founding my own training company to help others excel in their own real estate business, I have experienced much and I've been blessed beyond my dreams. There have been lots of highs and many lows and, in between them all, I became who I am today: someone who tries to be as real and down-to-earth as I was when I first came here.

In this culture of reality TV and fake celebrity, it's not easy to stay grounded. Everything is dramatized and hyped; very little seems real anymore. But when you come from nothing, staying grounded is absolutely vital to maintaining your very identity—it's something you fight to keep.

The first few years after I moved to this country I had so little; I prayed my electricity supply wouldn't be cut off. I couldn't pay my bills, and every day I hoped that my checks wouldn't bounce. Thankfully, I'm now in the happy position of not having to worry about those things, but that doesn't mean I will ever forget or deny the realities of my past. I'm glad I still think this way. If I didn't, I would be very far removed from everyday reality, and that is not a good spot to be in!

2. HOLDING ON AND LETTING GO

As I've said before, since I moved here, I have built a great life for myself and my family. But in the process, I had to leave my old life behind.

At our seminars and events, you'll usually see me dressed formally in a shirt and tie. What you might not notice is that I always wear Irish cuff links. These cuff links are a daily reminder of my past—a deliberate nod to my roots.

For an immigrant like me, there's a kernel of sadness and melancholy about the old country that is always present in the subconscious. It's a difficult thing to define, but every immigrant I know carries this sadness within them. To balance this emotion, however, there is also great joy present. I am so appreciative of all I have been blessed with here. Most of all, I have a desire and a feeling of duty and responsibility to contribute and give back however and whenever I can.

One of the ways I can do this is to share the valuable life lessons I have learned on my journey. Chief among these lessons is that to achieve success in your new homeland, there are certain things from your old life that you should hold on to and other things you need to let go of.

You should hold on to:

- A deep, abiding faith

- A sense of family

- A sense of humor

- An appreciation for a real quality of life versus a perceived "lifestyle"

You should let go of:

- The idea that you can't do what you're setting out to do

- Bitterness or jealousy of others

- People who hold you back

Holding on and letting go are two sides of the same coin that an immigrant holds in his hand. There is a fine line between turning your back on your old life and embracing your new. You must never forget your past and the lessons you've learned, but you should also wholeheartedly embrace the here and now and appreciate the opportunities in front of you. Doing so honors both your homeland and your new country.

3. PUTTING YOUR NAME TO IT

It's an old-fashioned idea, but when you put your name to something you do, whether in your personal or professional life, you stamp it with pride. Being able to hand-on-heart stand up and say that you and your business deliver in an exceptional way is an incredible gift, and not just to others but to yourself as well. As theologian Hosea Ballou said, "No one has a greater asset for his business than a man's pride for his work."

THE HARRY BUFFINI STORY

Can You Put Your Name to That?

Taking pride in your work not only serves your customer in the best way possible, it also nourishes your spirit. I was fortunate enough to learn this early in my life. As I've shared, my father is a fifth-generation painting contractor in our hometown of Dublin, and as a young boy I was taught the family trade along with my brothers. Our granddad, Harry, used to oversee our daily training and instruction. Both Dad and Granddad worked hard to always exceed their customers' expectations. In fact, they were so fastidious about their work that before leaving a job, they would change the lightbulbs and wash the windows so that no trace of paint or grime was left behind! That was the standard of care they delivered to their clients, and as a result, they received all of their work through word of mouth. They gave excellent customer service and received quality referrals as a consequence.

At the end of every working day, Granddad was famous for asking us Buffini brothers, "Can you put your name to that?" By asking this question, he was actually asking us if we were proud of the quality of our work. A subtle strategy, but extremely effective! One incident sticks in my mind.

We were painting a house and were almost finished for the evening. I was just putting away my paintbrush when I got a whiff of cigar smoke from the hallway—it was Granddad, with a fat cigar clamped between his two fingers as always, coming to talk to me before I left.

"So, Brian," he said, looking me dead in the eye, "can you put your name to that?"

I remember looking at the radiator that I'd just finished painting. I had knocked against it not long before and, although the client was probably never going to notice, chances were it would be a little streaked when it dried.

"I think it's a bit smudged," I replied, showing Granddad the paintwork. "When I come in tomorrow, I'm going to sand it down and do it over."

In my mind's eye, I can still see him nodding and smiling at me in response, saying very little, yet saying so much at the same time.

I often think of that moment. As one of my first mentors, my grandfather gave me a great gift. He instilled in me that we should always strive for excellence, and he empowered me to apply this principle throughout the rest of my life. Granddad didn't judge, and he wasn't looking for perfection—but he wanted me to do the best I could do in the time I had to finish a job. He taught me that always doing your best makes you feel really good about yourself. What a great life lesson!

The notion of "putting my name to it" is still the guiding principle of my life today. Personally, I strive to do my best for my wife and our six children. Spiritually, I work hard to put God's name to all of my intentions and actions. Professionally, I "put my name to it" every day. In fact, this one principle is the single most important premise on which the Buffini & Company referral method is based. Like my grandfather, here at Buffini & Company, we work to make excellence our minimum standard, and we teach the professionals who use our systems to do the same. Little did Granddad know that his philosophy of exceeding his clients' expectations helped his grandson build a fortune by impacting and improving the lives of hundreds of thousands of people! It's an incredible legacy and one I'm very proud to be part of.

My granddad's philosophy is in my blood. Every day I work, I remember where I came from and strive to put my name to whatever I do. I know what Granddad would have done with my opportunity, and I know he never would have settled for mediocrity! He had the Emigrant Edge . . . in spades!

HOW TO GET THE EDGE

The 21-Point Challenge for
Realizing Your Own Success

Introduction to Part Four

All you need is the plan, the road map, and the
courage to press on to your destination.

—EARL NIGHTINGALE

The Bible says that "faith without works is dead" (James 2:20 KJV). So are traits without application. Whenever I create an event, training program, coaching curriculum, or even a book, it's with the clear intention that those who participate will actually do something with the information. Now that you know what the seven Emigrant Edge principles are, you can use them in your own life and career to get a phenomenal head start. Your life is probably already pretty good in comparison to others'—now let's make it even better!

In this final section, I'll leave you with a detailed road map of how to do just that. I've made it even easier still by dividing each trait into three step-by-step subprinciples. That means you have to do twenty-one things to take you to the next level of success. Are you up to the challenge?

CHAPTER EIGHTEEN

How to Develop a Voracious Openness to Learn

No one was designed to settle for average in life. We all have the ability to excel in some way or another. Some people are gifted academically; others have a talent for sports or the arts. Still others have tremendous empathy and compassion and are outstanding parents, friends, or coworkers.

We can all be exceptional, but it takes strength and emotional toughness to stay motivated and positive in a critical environment. It's easy to be discouraged and settle for the "average" if the average is all we surround ourselves with.

A seed doesn't grow unless the conditions are good. It needs rich soil mixed with a balanced amount of sunshine and rain if it's to push its way up out of the dirt. It's the same with people. We can't develop properly if our growing conditions are poor. We have to give ourselves the very best chance to reach for the sky by providing the right environment for growth, or we will be stunted and never reach our full potential. How do we do this? We must police what we read, watch, and listen to.

CHALLENGE 1: UPGRADE YOUR INPUT

People often say to me, "There's no harm in trash TV, it's just a little fun." Now, I have to say I strongly disagree. Not only do trashy TV programs skew our perception of what's real and have a dumbing-down effect, they also make us unhappy and discontent with what we have in life.

I'm not saying I'm perfect, by the way! I'm not into reality TV, but I am into sports, and I can tell you I have to guard against getting caught in the trap of becoming a spectator instead of a player on the field. It's easy to get hooked on the countless twenty-four-hour sports or news channels available in this country. Of course, it's good to have an interest in sports or current affairs, but the difficulty comes when you spend your time goggle-eyed in front of the TV set instead of engaging in the real world. Before you know it, you're not in the game, you're just a couch potato!

The Internet can be the same trap. Social media can be great for a business, for example, but it can also become a distraction to the real work of building relationships, generating referrals, and making sales. How many times have you sat down at your desk to write an email or do some administrative task and then found yourself, hours later, gazing at the screen cross-eyed, wondering where the time has gone? It takes a second to get sucked into online surfing only to spend hours mindlessly trawling through websites that really offer nothing but mindless chatter and products you don't need. It's too easy to lose your focus and get hooked into "clickbait" articles that lead you down endless rabbit holes. You think you're harmlessly killing time surfing online, but you're actually contributing to the slow death of your own brain cells, your essence, and your very spirit. By "killing time," you're killing the very core of your life.

If your body and mind's intake is average, your general output will be average too. Our life experiences ultimately amount to whatever we pay most attention to, which is why quality reading content and television and radio programming is vital. There's a saying "You are what you eat." Well, I believe you are what you read, watch, and listen to. Unfortunately, many people these days read articles and blurbs totaling only 140 characters each. Their lives are spent scrolling through their Twitter feed. Their exposure to the outside world is condensed into one-second snapshots, and any real depth experienced from books and meaningful conversation is lost.

The fact is, if you want to have an edge in life, you have to focus on what you're feeding your brain. If you spend a lot of time on social media, watching trash TV, and viewing mindless material, then you need to reevaluate. (By the way, by making the effort to read books like this one, you already have the edge!)

To make sure you stay focused on things that help you grow, watch your:

- *Intake*—Be aware of what you read, watch, and listen to. Reduce your exposure to negativity. Take in daily doses of positive, life-affirming content and enroll in a lifestyle of learning. Be a student of life.

- *Associations*—Who builds you up? Who tears you down? You must seek out positive influences, role models, and mentors. You counsel your kids not to hang around with the wrong crowd—take your own advice!

- *Affirmations*—What do you say when you talk to yourself? It's very important to monitor the critical voice inside your head and encourage yourself instead. Be kind to yourself—treat yourself like you would treat a friend. If you heard someone criticizing a friend, you'd stand up and tell the person to stop, right? Give yourself the same respect. Build yourself up by affirming who you are, embracing the gifts God has given you, and celebrating your positive traits.

CHALLENGE 2: INCREASE YOUR PERFORMANCE THROUGH TRAINING AND ACCOUNTABILITY

Remember when you started your career and you couldn't wait to get going every day? Then, as your work became routine, you lost some of the enthusiasm and passion that used to drive you. That scenario can happen to everyone, but it doesn't have to stay that way. It's possible to recharge your energy and passion by enrolling in continuing education or training courses and by getting help from good accountability partners, mentors, and coaches.

> *Without continual growth and progress, such words as improvement, achievement, and success have no meaning.*
> —BENJAMIN FRANKLIN

Training

No one wants to stay stagnant in their career. We all have a natural inclination to want to grow and improve. But you can't expect to do so if you insist on staying exactly where you are and doing exactly the same thing.

Training has impacted me greatly throughout my career. After my mentor Gene Kullman took me to my first personal-growth seminar in 1989 and I was exposed to some of the great thought leaders of growth and personal development, my whole outlook on life and work changed. I realized that training was crucial to experiencing success and personal satisfaction. Over the years, I have attended classes on improving memory, managing time, and running a successful business, among many other subjects.

Continuing professional development is vital. It's important to keep up-to-date and current with your industry so that you can best advise your clients and provide the platinum service they deserve. To do so means setting aside the finances to cover the costs of new training—and that can be a challenge. When you're an entrepreneur, it's easy to put yourself at the bottom of your list of priorities. But if you fail to invest in yourself, you are the one who will lose out in the end as everyone else powers past you.

For example, when people ask me if they should come to one of our seminars, I reply with an unequivocal yes! If they say "I can't afford to," I ask them if they can afford not to. Now, that's not a fast-talking millionaire trying to make a quick buck, that's me giving an honest answer—it's advice I've taken myself. If you don't invest in yourself, then who will? You can't expect to grow and improve if you don't fertilize your soil regularly. Invest in yourself and believe that you're worth it.

Lifelong self-improvement is critical to success—it's your skills that pay the bills, so it's crucial to keep them fresh. If you lack the skills needed for today's market, the market will quickly render you redundant. The most successful people achieve success because they constantly invest in their own learning and training to stay innovative and important to their trade. That's what I did and what I continue to do, both professionally and personally.

In 2015, the average annual income of sales agents affiliated with the National Association of Realtors® was $29,560 per year. A Buffini & Company–coached agent earned an average of $336,698 a year, over eleven times more. What makes the difference? Training!

In summary,

- Ongoing professional training and development should never stop—and you should never let financial considerations stop your learning. There are countless training programs, courses, and resources you can subscribe to and tap into, even for free.

- Keep your skill set fresh or you will get stale. Your skills pay the bills! Do you want to be left behind, or do you want to be ahead of the curve?

- Always allocate 10 percent of your income to growth opportunities such as business conferences, training programs, business books, etc. This isn't a waste of valuable resources—it's a long-term investment in the health of your business.

Accountability

In his book *The Law of Happiness,* Henry Cloud describes a study in which scientists put a monkey into a high-stress environment to study the effects of stress on his brain. Then they kept the stress levels the same (bright lights, noise, etc.) and put a second monkey in the cage. Incredibly, they found that the first monkey's stress hormones reduced by about half, just because he got some companionship!

> *A man can learn only two ways; one by reading, and the other by association with smarter people.*
> —WILL ROGERS

It can be the same for us. Picture your professional life as that cage, full of setbacks and challenges. Why would you choose to soldier on alone, stressed and unhappy, instead of "buddying up" for support? When you're working to achieve your goals, spending time with like-minded people who share similar values really is a no-brainer. Birds of a feather flock together. Having someone in your personal and professional life who cares about how you're doing is inspiring, encouraging, and vastly stress-reducing. But those aren't the only benefits—it also makes you more accountable for your actions, and accountability is vital to success.

The truth is, the desire to achieve our potential is present in most of us, but unfortunately the will to live up to that desire is hard to maintain unless we have someone in our life to push and motivate us. Take exercising, for example. Committing to undertake an exercise regimen with a friend is always more successful than going solo. You're far less inclined to make excuses when you know someone is counting on you and expecting you to follow through on your agreement to keep fit together. Whether you really feel like it or not, that friend will come knocking on your door and drag you out for a run regardless of your mood, and vice versa. (The downside of accountability is that everyone wants it until they get it!)

When I ask audiences at our live events across the country how many of them believe they would achieve more if they were held accountable to daily tasks, everyone raises their hand. That's because we all know deep down that being held to account for our actions works. A little help never hurts, and we're better together than we are apart—I really can't emphasize that enough. You will never regret reaching out and getting help or support from someone (or helping someone else in turn). Doing so enhances your short- and long-term goal achievement, helps you

> *If you're the smartest person in the room, you're in the wrong room!*
> —UNKNOWN

track your success, and improves your performance. And, by the way, it's a lot more fun!

Accountability Partners

Everybody believes they're open to growth, but in reality, few really are. Most people want to change their circumstances, but they don't want to change themselves. The truth is, when we hear feedback that we don't like, many of us tend to bury our heads in the sand. We tell ourselves that the criticism doesn't apply to us, or the person who's giving it doesn't know what they're talking about. We tend to take it personally, instead of using it to improve. We create excuses for ourselves when we fail to perform as we want, and after a while it becomes easy to buy into those excuses instead of squaring up to and facing our own destructive behaviors and shortcomings.

We all have dreams, goals, and desires, but so often they are outside our comfort zone because they require change and a lot of work on our part. But if we truly want to live out a dream, *we* have to be different. If we want higher success in our business, *we* need to change and be accountable for our actions. This is where an accountability partner is invaluable. He or she helps you keep on track or get on a new one, remain focused on the process and your progress, and stay fired up and inspired to reach peak performance.

My good friend Joe Niego has been my accountability partner for most of my adult life, and I am his. If we hadn't had each other to rely on over the years, neither one of us would have achieved the level of success that we have. At the beginning of our careers, we would each set daily goals—how many calls we would make and personal notes we would write. Then, no matter how many hours we worked or how many transactions we did, we would call each other and report our lead-generation activities for that day. If one of us fell short, the other would ask for an explanation. Believe me, this blunt approach worked wonders for both of us!

Today, Joe and I still call each other often to check in that we're doing what we need to be doing . . . or to explain why not! There are no excuses—just frank and open discussion and encouragement. So, my advice to you is to find a Joe Niego in your own life to keep you accountable for your actions. It's a system that's extremely powerful and effective and a great way to refocus your energy and maximize your daily habits and routines.

Mentors

The concept of mentorship is as old as time. In Greek mythology, Mentor was the loyal friend and wise adviser of Ulysses and the teacher and guardian of Ulysses's son. Today, a mentor is still considered to be a guide, a role model, or a trusted adviser. Unlike an accountability partner, a mentor isn't one of your peers. He or she is typically someone who is further down the career path than you are, has experienced the success you hope to achieve, and is willing to share their insights with you. In business, a mentor might be a

> *My mentor said, "Let's go do it," not "You go do it." How powerful it is when someone says "Let's!"*
> —JIM ROHN

manager or an individual who has built significant success. In spiritual matters, a mentor could be a pastor or a member of your church community. In your family, a mentor can be a parent, an aunt, an uncle, or a grandparent—like my own grandfather was for me. For financial issues, a mentor could be a financial planner or an investment consultant you admire.

For many years, I have been incredibly blessed to have been mentored by some outstanding individuals from all walks of life. If I were to list all of the people who have taken the time to impart their wisdom to me, it would take all day. I have had, and continue to have, many incredibly giving and selfless mentors, all of whom have helped me during my life's journey. Everyone needs a mentor to get them to the next level in whatever they're doing—there are no exceptions to this rule.

Coaches

It's difficult to improve yourself alone. That's why personal trainers are so popular and why great athletic coaches are idolized by athletes and fans alike. The great tennis champion Althea Gibson—the first African American woman to win the world-famous Wimbledon championship—once said, "No matter what accomplishments you make, somebody helped you." How true that is.

To succeed, people need the grounding of an experienced mindset, but also the pick-me-up of motivation, ideas, and inspiration to stay focused and on track; and that's what a good coach offers. It doesn't matter if you're a legendary tennis player, the founder of a Fortune 500 company, or an ordinary Joe struggling with a personal issue or problem, everyone can benefit from the objective, expert viewpoint and advice of a coach.

A coach is a highly trained professional whose job it is to instruct, direct, and encourage you to achieve at your highest level. Unlike an accountability partner or a mentor, which is a volunteer role, a professional coach gets paid to motivate you. In the area of fitness, for example, an accountability partner is your workout buddy; your mentor is the legendary gym rat who is in great shape; and your coach is the personal trainer you hire to help you reach your health and fitness goals.

A coach can help you improve your skills, gain understanding of your strengths and weaknesses, and give you a fresh perspective. He or she holds you responsible for the fundamentals—the everyday practices that lead to success—but also fosters and encourages your self-belief.

Believing in yourself is hugely important. Often, we can subconsciously block success in our lives. We mistakenly think we can't achieve certain things because of doubts we have about our skills and capacity—beliefs that have been entrenched in us since childhood. That little voice of doubt inside can hold you back, but an effective coach can help you see that your growth can be unlimited and that you can achieve far more than you ever thought possible if you put your mind to it.

Now, getting coached isn't always easy. Often, we don't want to confront old ways of thinking or change our actions. We want to push forward, but we don't want to make changes in ourselves, perhaps because of fears or insecurities. But a good coach will challenge you to analyze your choices and help you make better ones. The sessions can feel like tough love at times because there is no hiding place! But then, if you keep doing things the old way, you will continue to get the same results.

Achieving success can be simple, but it's easy to overcomplicate the process. A good coach will help you focus on what's truly important and necessary and strip away the complexity that confuses you and bogs you down. He or she will help you to both streamline your efforts toward the simplest approach and create a workable, achievable plan for success.

A good coach will help you stay focused on the four things you need to succeed:

1. *Clear goals*: Here at Buffini & Company, our coached clients set goals—not only for business and finance, but for the other vital areas of their lives. After we help them create and get focused on their goals, we hold them accountable for the actions, decisions, habits, and routines they employ to reach those goals. Our coaches make sure our clients do more than just dream about what is possible— they help them achieve it!

2. *Good time management*: Good time management is absolutely key to achieving success. If you're disorganized, you are ineffective, simple as that! You must optimize your time, or it will slip through your fingers. In the real estate industry—my area of specialty and expertise—it's possible to work fifty hours a week and earn $50,000 in annual commissions or work fifty hours a week and earn $1 million in commissions. It isn't about intelligence or IQ, it's about what I call an "I Do" approach—through setting priorities. Identifying your pri-

orities is crucial to effective time management because it eliminates time wasted on less important tasks.

3. *A series of quick wins*: People get discouraged when they can't see progress. Coaches are great at getting people to focus on smaller steps to achieve small, quick wins. When you're winning, you experience a sense of accomplishment, your confidence builds, and you keep a tight focus on the endgame.

4. *Momentum*: Once you start to get a series of wins, it's important to keep the momentum going and build on it. Too many people get a few wins and then start to drift or coast. The truth is, when you're coasting, you're either slowing down or going downhill. The best way to maintain momentum is to revisit your goal and reengage with *why* you're doing what you're doing. A good coach will help you do this.

In short, having a coach is the surest way to uncover your path and clear your route to excellence. It isn't something that's done *to* you—it's a process whereby your coach walks *with* you. He or she works to help you realize your ambitions by removing the clutter that slows you down, allowing you to lean into your strengths more to draw out your best performance.

CHALLENGE 3: APPLY WHAT YOU LEARN

Having mentors and coaches over the years has completely transformed my life. When I was a young man, listening to the advice and wisdom of others set me on the path to success. But don't for a second think that just listening is ever enough—you must *apply* the teaching if you want your life to change! Have you ever bought exercise equipment but left it sitting in the box in the garage? Or have you ever attended a worthwhile and educational seminar, gotten all fired up, but then gone home and fallen into the same old habits and routines again?

We all have good intentions, but good intentions alone are worthless. The secret is in the application. You can have all the expertise, encouragement, and accountability possible, but you are still responsible for your own success. To get to where you want to go, you must take the direction and advice given to you, and then *implement it* in your own life. This is what I have done—and what I continue to do. No matter how successful you become, you can't afford to make the mistake of thinking you know it all or you have reached the pinnacle of success—there's always more to learn and more to do.

I am constantly being reminded of the importance and value of ongoing coaching. In a recent episode of my podcast, for example, I shared a story of climbing one of the tallest peaks in the Canadian Rockies with my eldest son, AJ, when he was fifteen.

Every year, I take some time out to exercise hard, eat well, and recharge. I call it my "walkabout." That year, AJ asked if he could come on my walkabout with me. Thinking it would be some great bonding time with him, I happily agreed and we set off on a trip to the Canadian Rockies together. However, after a few days of what I thought was energetic hiking and working out, my very athletic son was already bored!

"Dad, can't we do something a little more exciting?" he said.

So I asked around for a few recommendations and that's when

we heard about Nils, a world-famous mountaineer. This guy's day job was to take high-net-worth individuals heli-skiing in the Himalayas. Now, I don't ski, but when we were told we could hike a glacier instead, I was sold.

However, as soon as we climbed into the helicopter that was flying us to the glacier, I started to worry about what I had agreed to. My worry intensified when Nils shouted above the noise of the chopper that when we reached the "drop zone," we had to make sure to jump and roll to our right or we'd get struck by the helicopter's rotors. There was now zero doubt in my mind—I was definitely out of my comfort zone. When the time came, we jumped and rolled as instructed. Success! But as I crouched in the snow and watched the helicopter disappear over the horizon, I still had a sense of dread. However, because AJ was with me—and we were with a trustworthy guide—I tried not to let my nerves show.

We took off up the mountain in single file, strapped to each other by a rope. The ascent started out okay, but the terrain soon began to get steeper and more challenging. Then we came to what Nils called a "crevasse." From what I saw before me, I knew that getting across that crack in the ice wasn't going to be fun. Nils talked us through what we needed to do and then led the way, making it look easy. AJ went next—again, he made it look simple. Then it was my turn. Let me tell you, it was very cold on that mountain, but at that moment in time I was sweating! I said a prayer, jumped across the crevasse, body-slammed against the wall of ice opposite, and immediately started to slide downward. My new hiking boots suddenly felt like they weighed a ton; they weren't gripping the ice properly and I couldn't find a good foothold. My life flashed before my eyes. This was it. Above me, AJ was urging me to climb. But, fearing I was going to drag him down with me into the 2,000-foot drop below, I did what Nils had explicitly ordered us not to do—I unhooked myself from AJ.

I was now totally freaked out. And, to make things worse, I realized that my fear of heights was more intense than I'd thought. It was at that moment that Nils called to me. He looked me straight in the eye. He could sense my fear and panic, but he was as cool as a cucumber.

"Brian," he said calmly, "you're a great coach. You help people climb mountains every day. Today, I'm going to help you. Do exactly as I say and everything will be fine."

I knew I had to trust him if I wanted to get out of the mess I had gotten myself into. And that's what I did. It took every ounce of courage and adrenaline in me, but I made it to the top of that mountain that day by literally following in his footsteps, inch by inch. When I got to the top, I wasn't on cloud nine. Instead, I felt embarrassed. I had made a fool of myself in front of my son, I had let myself down, and I had exposed some serious weaknesses in my fitness and athletic capabilities. But then Nils turned to me and said, "That was one of the best days ever—it was so inspiring!"

I was stunned. "What are you talking about?" I said. "I was terrible!"

"Brian," he said, "let me tell you something. Taking an experienced mountain climber up here isn't fulfilling to me. But to help you get over your fears and limitations and achieve something that years from now you're going to be proud of? That's why I do what I do!"

It was a seminal moment in my life because I realized that's also why I do what I do. That trip did more than challenge my fear of heights while bonding with my teenage son; it helped me remember why I love coaching people. It's why our world-class business coaches love what they do too. We enjoy being able to help our clients face their fears and limitations so they can achieve their goals, reach a high level of success, and live the good life. The truth is, the best coaches can help you identify and tap into your full potential. They'll help you set goals, stay on track, think through approaches to challenges, and give you honest feedback when you need it most. Most important, like Nils, they'll encourage you to keep going when you're feeling discouraged or tempted to quit. It's all about developing the mind-sets, motivation, and methodologies to succeed on whatever mountain *you* want to climb.

CHAPTER NINETEEN

How to Grow a Do-Whatever-It-Takes Mind-Set

Having a do-whatever-it-takes mind-set is important, but unless you also have a solid action plan based on a set of written goals, you'll get nowhere. Every year, countless small businesses across America fail because of this simple oversight. The problem isn't lack of passion, it's lack of focus and clear direction. We all care about nurturing our companies and serving our clients, but often we're so busy dealing with the day-to-day pressures of juggling our workloads that we don't stop to think about where we are actually going. Instead of trying to identify and then focus on our ultimate goals, we spend our

> *If you fail to plan, you plan to fail.*
> —ZIG ZIGLAR

days fighting fires and battling never-ending to-do lists with little to show for our time. How many of us feel like hamsters on a wheel, running as fast as we can but not really getting anywhere? Sound familiar? When we don't know where we're going, it's no wonder we can become frustrated and disillusioned, even plagued with serious business problems. As the old saying goes, "If you aim at nothing, you'll hit it with amazing accuracy."

Writing a set of goals can change all this. Don't worry—this doesn't have to be complicated and you don't need a Harvard degree to do it. At heart, it's simply a map of where you want to go. Just like an architect needs to create a set of detailed drawings before construction begins, everyone needs a blueprint to refer to when building a solid foundation for success. It's a way of getting from one place to another—just like an immigrant has to get from one place to another in order to make it in a new country.

CHALLENGE 4: BE A GOAL-GETTER

I remember writing my first goal like it was yesterday. I was attending an event where the great author and motivational speaker Lou Tice was a guest. From the stage, he told everyone in the audience how to set a goal by projecting themselves into the future. He advised us to write our goal as if it had already happened, detailing what would be the downsides if we didn't accomplish the goal and the upsides if we did.

At the time, our firstborn, AJ, was six months old. I hadn't been back to Ireland in four years and Beverly had never visited my homeland. So I wrote that I wanted to get the whole family together back home. I made my vision extremely detailed and descriptive. We'd rent a farmhouse in County Clare, go for long walks, have family meals, and spend real quality time together. Then I began to write out the benefits of achieving this goal and the consequences of non-completion. It was when I wrote down that my parents could pass away and never get to see their first grandchild that my mind was made up. I decided I was going to make this vision happen, come hell or high water. I left that conference and went straight to the travel agency and booked the trip. I put it on an American Express card because I didn't have the money to pay for it up front, as we had just purchased a house and had used up all of our available cash. I calculated that there were twenty-two days until the bill came in, and then I had thirty days to pay it. I had fifty-two days. I went to work.

Up until then, I had never sold more than six homes in a month. The month I wrote the goal, I sold thirteen homes. The month after, I sold twelve. When I tell this story, people often ask me where the leads suddenly came from. The truth is, they were on my desk. They were written on 3×5 cards and scrawled on scraps of paper where I had scribbled contact details of people I had meant to follow up with. I was literally surrounded by leads. The thing was, at that time I had gotten a little comfortable but hadn't real-ized it. Ultimately, when I set the goal and achieved it, I changed forever because I broke through a preconceived notion that six deals a month was a huge number. That figure used to be my maxi-mum, but once I set that goal, that ceiling became a floor. Once I did thirteen deals in a month, I thought to myself, *You know, my arms and legs didn't fall off. I can handle this.* That set in motion what has been a lifetime of goal setting. And the same thing has hap-pened for Buffini & Company.

One word of warning here—you have to be careful not to get so carried away with your goals for the future that you forget to do what's needed for the here and now! It's great to be ambitious and set goals for future growth, but you shouldn't lose sight of what's in front of you either. Make sure you handle the responsibilities you are currently tasked with. I believe that the person who can't take care of $100 can't take care of $1,000 and will fail miserably with $1 million.

Think of the Bible story of David and Goliath. This shepherd boy spent years diligently guarding his father's sheep in the hills of Bethlehem, going mostly unnoticed by everyone. When the call then came to protect his own people from the giant Goliath, David didn't flinch. He stepped forward with great heart and courage and felled Goliath with killer aim to the forehead using one small rock. His moment had arrived—and his years of quiet but unflinching care of those flocks, diligently protecting them from danger, had prepared him for his date with destiny.

People are forever waiting for their "big break" or for their circumstances to change. But if you don't do the work that's in front of you right now, then you'll never get to where you want to go. As I've shared, one of my first jobs in America was selling T-shirts to tourists off a cart on Crystal Pier in Pacific Beach. Was it my dream job? No. Did I have to hustle every day to make sales? Yes. And let me tell you, I worked hard! But even though it was hard work, I still enjoyed it. I saw that job as an opportunity—a step in the right direction toward what I ultimately wanted. I had dreams, but I also knew to concentrate on the here and now. It's a funny thing, but because I had the Emigrant Edge, I really engaged with my customers and discovered that many of the tourists actually wanted sweatshirts, not T-shirts. The folks visiting from Arizona were cold in California in the evenings! Now, no one else on the pier was providing sweatshirts, so I quickly managed to source some, and in no time business was booming!

In retrospect, that job was tough, but it taught me a lot: how to interact with, connect with, and listen to people so I could find out what they really wanted and then provide it for them—the first rule of sales and good customer service. I can also honestly say that working on that pier helped the future me to stand on a stage in front of thousands of people years later and help them reach their goals. From little acorns!

So if your goal is to have your own restaurant someday, but you're currently stuck washing dishes in the kitchen, don't get resentful or neglectful of your job or position. Remember, the fastest route to get to where you want to go is to be the greatest dishwasher that your establishment has ever seen. If you tackle your daily work with energy and enthusiasm, whether it's washing dishes or selling real estate, it will get you noticed and set you on the path to success. We can often miss the fact that tomorrow is built on today. If you can't be good at what you're doing now, how are you ever going to be good at a more challenging and demanding role in the future? You can alter your life by altering your attitude . . . and by writing goals!

You should write:

- *Short-term goals* to get started. You might decide to make a certain number of calls before lunchtime every day for the next month, for example.

- *Midterm goals* to keep going. You could aim to clear any debts within a year, perhaps.

- *Long-term goals* to give hope. Who says it's unrealistic to dream of buying a yacht and sailing around the world? Hope is vital for the human spirit. Chip away at your goals in a systematic and focused way and anything is possible.

A written goal has three key advantages:

1. *It clarifies what you really want.* Sometimes the idea of even trying to articulate what it is that you really want—from business or from life—can feel overwhelming. To get the ball rolling, try reflecting on what it is that you *don't* want. Perhaps you want to get rid of the pressure or chaos that surrounds you, or to work less and earn more. Devote even five or ten minutes from your busy day to thinking about this and then writing down what comes to mind. The very act of writing down these broad-stroke ideas will inspire you and, in no time, what you *do* want will become crystal clear.

2. *It creates objectives on which to focus your energy.* A lot of people suffer from almost crippling feelings of lethargy. Why? Because they have no focus! It's impossible to tap into your energy or use your unique gifts when you lack this crucial element of success. A goal identifies core objectives and gives you the ability to harness your energy far more effectively than ever before. Ordinary people can achieve extraordinary results if they know what they want and concentrate on working to achieve it.

3. *It becomes a lighthouse in the storm.* We all know that life isn't always smooth sailing. Everyone encounters challenges and disappointments, whether in business or in life at large. In difficult times, a goal is like a lighthouse—a beacon that guides you through the choppy waters and back safely to the shore, where you can fulfill your potential and realize your dreams.

CHALLENGE 5: BE RELENTLESS

Potential is defined as "a latent or underdeveloped power that has not yet come to pass." Everyone has potential, but many of us subconsciously prevent ourselves from tapping into it. That's right—we're often the biggest saboteurs of our own success. What's to blame? Fear. Whether we're afraid of failing or succeeding, we can let fear dominate our thinking. We waste our energy worrying, doubting, and zoning in on thoughts that limit our beliefs. We stick with unproductive routines and habits that inhibit our progress and prevent us from reaching our goals, if we've set goals at all. Or we work in isolation, away from the motivation and camaraderie of other high-achieving individuals. Luckily, it's never too late to tap into the greatness that you were destined to achieve. If you want to live your best life, be *relentless* in your pursuit of it! Face your fears, change your mind-set, and adopt the habits that will lead you to success.

Compete with Yourself

The definition of the word *compete* is "to strive to excel or outdo others." When you're in competition with others, you naturally compare yourself to them. However, comparison can be the ultimate joy stealer and can lead to negativity, cynicism, and low self-esteem. For example, when a team wins the World Cup in soccer, the commentator asks, "Are they as good as the 1972 Brazil team?"

Everyone is far too concerned with what others are doing. My advice? Stop trying to keep up with the Joneses and work at being the best version of *you*. Compete with yourself first before you're tempted to compare yourself to anyone else.

Competing with yourself means fulfilling and utilizing all your God-given abilities. To do this, you have to understand and work with your own gifts. We all have strengths and weaknesses. There are things we find simple to do and there are things that just don't come naturally to us. The key to finding a successful balance is to leverage and utilize the strengths that you've been blessed with while developing and managing your shortcomings.

> *Talent you have naturally. Skill is only developed by hours and hours and hours of beating on your craft.*
> —WILL SMITH

How you play to your strengths and shore up your weaknesses is in direct proportion to how much you will grow, both personally and in business. Here at Buffini & Company, before a client begins our coaching program, he or she completes a Heritage Profile. This profile is a real eye-opener! It helps our clients understand their own unique makeup and the inherent personal abilities and gifts that they possess.

If you really understand yourself at a core level, then you can empower yourself to become the best version possible by acting on that awareness. You can learn how to understand and then leverage your unique abilities both personally and professionally, and concentrate on doing more of what you excel at and less of what you don't.

Know Your Strengths

Everyone can say what they're bad at, but what are your gifts? Often, your strengths can be difficult to identify because they're so natural to you that you don't recognize them as anything special. What is it that you've repeatedly done well since you were a child? What comes easy to you that others find hard? These are some of the ways you can identify your talents. In fact, the first time you might realize you have a gift is when you see someone struggling with a task and you can't understand why they're finding it so difficult. It can take time and hard work to figure out what your strengths are, but identifying—and then using them—is vital to success.

Play To and Leverage Your Strengths

Don't get distracted by what your competitors are doing or chase activities that don't resonate with who you are. Instead, leverage what you're good at. If you're a people person, for example, then maximize this in every way you can. Zero in and focus on your strengths—work hard at them, practice them, and nurture them. Once you've identified your talents, the next step is to identify skills in each area. Talent with skill is a recipe for greatness. The most successful people find out what their strengths are, match them with something they enjoy doing, and then go and do it!

Identify and Shore Up Your Weaknesses

We're all human, so it goes without saying that we all have weaknesses. You don't have to focus on your shortcomings, but to be ultimately successful, you must evaluate what they are and then regulate them. By that I mean you should take an honest assessment to identify and acknowledge your weaknesses, and then put a support system in place. That might mean hiring an assistant, for example, or leaning on other professionals for advice and help. As President Theodore Roosevelt once said, "The best leader is the one who has sense enough to pick good people to do what needs to be done, and self-restraint enough to keep from meddling with them while they do it."

Just because you're not good at something doesn't mean that you get a hall pass, by the way. You must delegate and systematize your shortcomings, yes, but you don't have license to abdicate total responsibility because, in the end, you are responsible for your actions.

Play to Win

Once you've worked on yourself, then you can turn your attention to what others are doing in your field. In sports, we often see copycat syndrome—where a winning team gets studied by other teams, who then adjust their strategy to model that of the champion. It's smart business to survey successful competitors—see what they are doing that works and why, and figure out where you need to improve and how you can raise your game. The point is not to compare, but to observe, evaluate, and apply what your successful competitor is doing to your own working model.

CHALLENGE 6: BE ALL IN ON YOUR GOALS

Most of us set goals in January . . . and most of us forget all about them a few months later! Just try to find a free treadmill at the gym in January or February. Impossible! By March, however, most people have lost the motivation to sweat for thirty minutes a few times a week, and there are empty treadmills as far as the eye can see.

While the initial surge of motivation is enough to keep us on track for the first week or two, it's not enough to sustain us over longer periods of time. Often we become so busy juggling our day-to-day commitments that our goals seem more out of reach than ever. When that happens, you must remind yourself of your prescription for success. Are you clear about what you're trying to accomplish? Is your target distinct and measurable? Is your time frame realistic? Review your monthly, weekly, and daily written goals. If you're struggling, a good coach can help to keep those goals in front of you so you don't drift off course.

A top tip is to keep your plan simple! Leonardo da Vinci once said, "Simplicity is the ultimate sophistication." When it comes to reaching your goals, nothing could be truer. Many people struggle because they don't have the confidence and humility to keep the path to their goals simple. To succeed, you don't need intricate tactics or expensive, sophisticated tools; you just need a solid plan and a commitment to be all in. That way you can be a goal-getter with purpose and focus. Here are some more tips:

Schedule It Out

If something's not in the schedule, it just doesn't happen. We can have the best of intentions when it comes to getting things done, but intentions alone won't ensure we get to where we want to go. A good schedule prevents you from getting distracted by a never-ending to-do list and neglecting your priorities. Remember: The bulk of your day must be committed to activities that will help you achieve your goals. Review your time-management processes and determine if your schedule is truly effective. By the way, remember to schedule some "me time" in there too—that's nonnegotiable unless you want to experience exhaustion and burnout.

Create and Stick to Your To-Do List

Daily habits are critical to financial success, most especially in how we manage our time. It's all too easy for hours to slip by answering emails and becoming distracted by social media. To keep on track, create and diligently stick to a to-do list. Schedule appointments and build time blocks for high-priority activities in your daily planner. If you make these tasks nonnegotiable, you will consistently achieve your priorities.

Remember Routines

In a world where we're faced with what seems like a million decisions every day, routines and habits minimize the choices we have to make. The more automatic something is, the more likely it is to happen, and with minimal effort. You may think you're not a disciplined person, but you already have routines in place in your daily life. It's just that they've become so ingrained that you no longer notice them, like brushing your teeth. A good coach will be able to advise you on replacing any negative, draining routines with positive, proactive ones.

Track and Measure

If you have no formula to measure your success, then you will have nothing by which to monitor your progress—or lack of it. Write down your goals, determine what you have to accomplish every day to reach them, and then consistently track your activities. This is a great way to see what you've achieved and how far you've come, helping to keep you fired up and motivated. If you don't track your progress, then you can easily drift off course.

Many distractions and obstacles will come up. Often, our attempts to form good habits can be overwhelmed by the volume of things on our to-do list. Sometimes it can feel like you're constantly putting out fires. This is something you need to learn to cope with, because ironically, the more successful you get, the more fires there will be to put out.

The key to handling hiccups like this is to deal with them on your terms. Build some time into your schedule to address them. When you relegate difficulties to a specific time block, they won't hijack your entire day. Since you know you'll deal with them during a certain time, you won't have to divert your attention from the more productive tasks that are calling for your attention. Being proactive about controlling the time you spend problem-solving is a small step that will have a big impact on your success.

I can't overstate how important it is to write down your goals. In my life, I have experienced three major turning points. The first was the day I began to get to know God, the second was the day I met Beverly, and the third was the day I started writing down my goals. Those are the three events that turned me from the boy I was into the man I am now. Today, I can check off my personal accomplishments and the achievements of my business against specific goals that I wrote down. That's why, for the past twenty years, at every seminar I've ever presented, not only have I taught people the importance of goal setting, but I actually have them take time during the event to write down goals.

How do you eat an elephant?
One bite at a time!
—ANONYMOUS

If you're struggling with goal writing, try this simple exercise that I have taught to thousands of real estate professionals who use our referral systems every year. Make a list of ten-day goals, writing down one specific item in each of these areas: *business, financial, family, spiritual,* and *personal.* At the end of the ten-day period, your life won't have miraculously changed. However, you will have had a good stretch of solid productivity and progress, and you'll have taken a major step in the right direction toward future success. It only takes twelve ten-day stretches to optimize an incredible one-third of your year. By doing this simple exercise, you will begin to create the habit of winning. There's power in a goal, and when you have one, there's power in you!

CHAPTER TWENTY

How to Develop a Willingness to Outwork Others

Being willing to outwork others doesn't just mean putting your nose to the grindstone and keeping it there until the job is done. Yes, you should apply all-in energy and effort if you want to achieve success, but a willingness to outwork others also means having the discipline to be consistent, the ambition to become exceptional, and the intelligence to leverage the rest/run cycle.

This principle is so important that this is the longest chapter in the book. When you put this guide into action, you'll see amazing results . . . and if you don't do it, you'll compound your customers' dissatisfaction. Let me explain.

CHALLENGE 7: BE CONSISTENT

As a parent, one of the hardest things to do is to be consistent with your children. It's also one of the most important. Kids thrive on routine and consistency. As they grow, learn, and develop, they are presented with many changes on a daily basis. They need to know what to expect in some areas of their young lives if they're to feel secure and loved. They like predictability about certain things because it makes them feel safe. If the ground is always shifting under their feet, they can become unsure of their place in the world and even mistrustful of other people. For children, inconsistency equals anxiety.

> *Do everything with character and integrity and practice persistent consistency in everything you do.*
> —TOM ZIGLAR

Predictability also informs their behavior. If consequences aren't predictable—if they can't tell what will happen if they use bad language or don't do their homework, for example—then their good behavior can deteriorate. Children need structure and boundaries: When is bedtime? What happens if they break curfew? What will be the result if they don't tidy their room? If they aren't sure what the consequences will be because the rules keep changing, the outcome will ultimately be unfavorable for everyone.

As parents, it's difficult to be consistent, because guess what? . . . we're only human! Sometimes it's just easier to pick up after our kids instead of nagging them to clean up. But consistency pays off handsomely in the long run because it helps our kids learn how to be responsible, well-adjusted adults who handle challenges well and go on to make a valuable contribution in the world. So it's important to make being consistent a habit—we have to become consistent with our consistency!

It's not just in our personal lives that consistency is important. It's the same in business. When you're consistent in your dealings with clients and customers, they learn they can rely on you. They know they can trust you to look after their best interests and that you are always on the lookout for helpful ways to serve them. The relationships you build with your clients are vital to the long-term growth and success of your business.

In the real estate industry, client relationships are the lifeblood of a business. But, unfortunately, many real estate agents don't realize this. They close a transaction and then lose touch with their clients immediately after. Ask a homeowner for the name of their agent, and most of them can't think of it because most never hear from their agent again once the sale has been completed. In fact, one of the biggest complaints buyers and sellers have is that their agents didn't stay in contact. Unfortunately, most agents think that once the ink is dry their job is done. But in reality, the relationship with the client has only just begun.

This philosophy applies to many other industries too. The initial sale is only the beginning of the relationship; staying in touch with your clients provides the opportunity to become a trusted adviser.

You can find ways to serve your clients long after the transaction has closed by:

- Being consistent with your marketing

- Finding a need to fill

- Connecting your clients with trusted professionals in your network

- Listening

These things not only show your clients that you care, they're also essential for building the foundations of strong relationships. By the way, they also sow seeds for future business and generate a consistent stream of leads.

By being consistent in your transactions with clients, you will:

1. *Build Trust*: That feeling of being able to consistently rely on someone—whether it's a family member, friend, colleague, customer, or business associate—builds trust. Even a small thing like sending marketing flyers, calling to touch base, or sending an email with useful information for their business can be a building block for establishing trust with your clients. Consistent care and contact reminds your clients that you are always on hand to assist them, which builds and strengthens your relationships for the long term.

2. *Create a Successful Habit*: The process of becoming consistent has an interesting consequence—you'll develop a good habit. That's right; as you connect with your clients and complete your lead-generating activities, doing so will become a habit. The good thing about habits is that activities that used to take concerted effort become automatic, and when they're automatic, you will feel strangely unsettled if you *don't* complete them.

3. *Lay the Groundwork for Future Referrals*: Being consistent is not only a habit successful people possess for maintaining a strong client base, it's also a way to build on those relationships to gain reliable leads for the future. In the real estate industry, many agents spend thousands of dollars purchasing leads from online sources, but the real professionals simply develop relationships with their clients. To lead and grow a solid business, be consistent, build trust, and generate the leads that help your business thrive.

When I first started out, I had to learn and work at being consistent myself. I used to be disorganized in my daily routines—consistency was not my forte! But that all changed when I met Dr. Alex Lackey, named in the "Who's Who" as the Most Organized Man in America. One day, we arranged to meet for coffee. He was waiting for me when I barreled through the coffee shop door. I was running late as usual because I had been scurrying all over town meeting clients. I apologized and bought him a coffee, and we sat down together.

During our conversation, he asked me, "Do your clients mind you being late, Brian?"

I had to admit I hadn't thought that much about it. I wasn't ever *very* late—I usually ran behind by only a few minutes. Then he said something to me that forever changed how I viewed this.

"We are always trying to show our clients that they can trust us and that we have their best interests at heart," he said. "There's what I call a trust account between us. When you show up late, you make a withdrawal from that trust account. Being on time is a small detail, but details build trust." From then on, I was never late again. In fact, now I'm usually early!

If the only consistent thing about your habits and routines is inconsistency, then something has to radically change for you to experience a breakthrough in this area. You don't have to throw all your current behaviors out the window and adopt new and better ones. In fact, trying to make big, sweeping changes like that is the best way to fail. As we know, the person who loses the most weight in the long run isn't the sugar-loving couch potato who suddenly swears off junk food and starts running five miles a day. He may start out strong for a few days, but he will quickly lose momentum and soon be reaching for the chocolate cake or putting off workouts within a few weeks. But the individual who simply replaces an afternoon soda with an apple day after day is the one who makes the greatest strides over time.

If you want to improve your habits, start small. Then once you've formed one good habit, work on another one. Those small, incremental steps will eventually help you develop good habits so they become a new way of life. The key is to be consistent.

CHALLENGE 8: BECOME EXCEPTIONAL

Once you've earned people's trust by being consistent, then you want to wow them by being exceptional. That's why, no matter what job you have, you want to be the very best at it. Being exceptional is not about being typical, it's about being unusual. One of my favorite words to describe exceptional is *uncommon*.

In his bestseller, *Uncommon: Finding Your Path to Significance,*

NFL Hall of Fame coach Tony Dungy shares his approach to helping teams, players, and leaders become exceptional. The title of the book comes from a quote by former University of Minnesota coach Cal Stoll, who told Dungy as a freshman football player: "Success is uncommon, therefore not to be enjoyed by the common man. I'm looking for uncommon people."

Uncommon people are rare, which is why, when you meet one, you remember them. This is how you want your customers to remember you.

When we at Buffini & Company teach our clients how to generate referrals from their customers, one of the things we share with them is to do the unexpected extras. Of course, you have to understand that these *unexpected* extras only have relevance if you are doing the *expected* consistently. Being exceptional is built on the bedrock of consistency. By doing what's expected consistently you create trust; then you build upon that trust by doing what's exceptional.

> *It is the service we are not obliged to give that people value most.*
> —J. C. PENNEY

When you're exceptional, people talk about you. When you're exceptional, you're likely to get promoted. When you're exceptional, your clients refer you to other customers.

Make Your Customers Feel Valued

Business owners must remember that customers don't check their feelings at the door when they enter your place of business. Whether it's the restaurant that fails to make things right after a customer receives poor service or a bad meal, or the store that seems to care less when there's an issue with a product, if customers believe they haven't been appreciated, they will feel deeply dissatisfied. Being unappreciated cuts to the quick, so after experiencing disappointment, who wants a second helping of a bitter pill? With so much choice and competition in the marketplace, customers will simply go elsewhere—and take their friends with them. As the saying goes: "Your customer may not thank you for making mistakes, but your competitor will!"

Ask yourself: What standards of behavior and service do you provide to your customers? Do you serve them in such a way that it builds up the relationship or tears it down? Making customers feel valued needs to be at the center of all you do. The relationship between personal value and the bottom line is a critical one. Businesses that are just average—or below—will always pay the biggest price in the end.

Many corporate businesspeople operate under the illusion that "creating value" means catering to the shareholders. But this is a fatal mistake. Your most important assets are your customers. Their desires and needs should be the focus of a business's endeavors—they shouldn't get lost in the corporate shuffle and frantic race for gaining a profit at any cost. My next story illustrates this.

I like to take my family home to Ireland as often as possible. One year, I researched a lot of locations to find the perfect place that would suit all our needs. At the top of the list of activities we wanted to do was horseback riding. From a very young age, my daughter Anna has been a horse fanatic, and I wanted to take her somewhere she could indulge in her passion. After hours of searching, I found the perfect place for us to go. It was a little more grandiose than where we'd normally stay—it was an estate hotel in the middle of the countryside with a world-class golf course, fly-fishing, an indoor pool, and equestrian facilities. All six of my kids were over the moon when they saw where we were going, but Anna was especially so. "I'm going to ride every single day!" she said to me excitedly.

Before we left, I called to book the riding lessons in advance, but the hotel staff assured me this wasn't necessary—it would all be sorted out on arrival.

Three weeks later, we arrived at the hotel to find a very different story. The stables were closed and, despite what I'd been told, there were no horses to ride . . . and there wouldn't be for the entirety of our stay. I reminded the staff that I had tried to call ahead to book the lessons but had been informed there was no need to. I also let them know the primary reason we had picked their location was due to the equestrian facilities. What did I get in return? A dronish, non-heartfelt response of "Sorry, there just aren't any horses available."

"Is there any way you can help me out? Are there equestrian facilities within driving distance I could take the kids to each day?" I asked.

"I'm not aware of any" was the reply.

"Has this situation ever happened before?" I asked.

"Yes, several times, sir" was the reply.

"And it never occurred to you to find an alternate situation for your guests?"

As you can imagine, I was shocked—this was far from the Irish hospitality I knew and loved—and it was costing me an arm and a leg to boot. But there was worse to come.

Next, we decided to go swimming. At the hotel pool, however, we were told we would have to purchase bathing caps to wear, and that all children under twelve would have to wear armbands—another added cost. My kids have grown up swimming like dolphins in their own backyard pool, but now I had to buy them rubber caps and plastic floaties. We had traveled five thousand miles to find that not only could the kids not go horseback riding, but now I had to pay through the nose to bring everyone swimming! I couldn't believe it.

The last straw was when I invited my dad and his best friend to drive to the countryside and play the "world-class" golf course. Not only was it one of the most expensive green fees I had ever paid, but the last of the nickel-and-diming occurred as we went out to the driving range. They wanted us to pay for range balls *and* score cards. Everything was an à la carte upcharge. That night we made the decision to check out and head west for a true taste of Irish hospitality. Thankfully, we ended up having a wonderful vacation in the end, despite the poor start.

That resort had a culture of not valuing the customer. I found out later that during the Celtic Tiger years (when the Irish economy grew enormously) they were booked up every night and increased their rates significantly. But the growth in their business led to a serious disconnect from caring for and valuing their guests. On my last trip home to Ireland following the country's recent Great Recession, I learned of major layoffs that had taken place at the establishment and that prices were exactly half of what they had been five years earlier.

My advice to a business that's experiencing growth? Don't get fooled by apparent prosperity or success. Even a turkey can fly in a hurricane. Stop valuing your customers and one day your business will pay the price.

As an aside: Since that time Anna continued to pursue her love of horses and went on to become a US Dressage National Champion! Wouldn't it have been nice for that hotel to have been able to boast that the number one young rider in North America once used its hotel stables? Sadly, the hotel's management wasn't concerned with making its clientele feel valued—it was only concerned with meeting its bottom line.

There's an old adage in sales: Find 'em, fleece 'em, and forget 'em. This crude approach perfectly describes how some organizations used to (and still do) treat their clients. They have no interest in developing a relationship with their customers or offering them lasting value. They're just in their jobs for the money. Now this approach may net a profit in the short term, but because it's a one-off tactic, it makes no provision for future opportunities. Discounting clients once a transaction has been completed means that the door is closed on any future prospects that may exist. You may gain in the short term but your loss will be long term. If a business is focused purely on the checks and isn't invested in its customers, then customers will naturally treat that business not as a trusted adviser or provider but as a commodity—one that can be discarded without a second thought.

It's a fact of life that things can go wrong—nobody is perfect—so there will be times when mistakes are made. But in business, what matters most is that when a problem arises it is acknowledged, an apology is forthcoming, and efforts are made to rectify the situation quickly and efficiently. As Zig Ziglar said, "Statistics suggest when customers complain, business owners and managers ought to get excited about it. The complaining customer represents a huge opportunity for more business."

At Buffini & Company, we quickly became the fastest-growing business in our space. In the ten consecutive years since our founding, we grew a minimum of 40 percent a year. Needless to say, during that time frame we experienced some growing pains. As fanatical as I am about customer service, that was an area where the ball got dropped. But we didn't hide from the problems—we addressed them the very best we could as soon as we realized there were issues. When a mistake happens you must apologize, make it right, and make sure the customer knows they're highly valued. Not only will they appreciate it, but they'll also extend more grace to you. Everybody likes to be around the energy and enthusiasm of growth; people just want to know that, during that growth, you're committed to excellence and that ultimately you're going to find a way to make any wrongs right again.

It is said that, on average, it takes twelve positive experiences to make up for one unresolved negative experience. This is why it's critical to resolve any disputes quickly and in the customer's favor. The business that treats a customer as part of the problem and not part of the solution will suffer—they will never be referred to a customer's family, friends, or colleagues, and word will spread that problems are handled badly. Future customers may hold off doing business with you if they hear through the grapevine or online that after-sales care is lackluster or nonexistent. There's no telling how much valuable business is lost as a consequence.

If you show your customer that you truly care when a problem arises, you will demonstrate real value. Customers don't expect a business to be perfect, but they do expect to be treated well in times of trouble. A simple but heartfelt and timely apology, coupled with a genuine effort to rectify whatever went wrong, works wonders!

Go the Extra Mile

According to the dictionary, going the extra mile means "to make more effort than is expected of you." In business, this principle can't be just an occasional or an ad hoc attitude. The relationship of trust that companies strive to create with customers is built one interaction at a time across a wide platform of communication highways, including social media and personal contact. This means that the "extra-mile" culture can only be achieved if everyone—from boardroom to front line—is on the same page and passionately believes that the company's primary purpose is to put customers first. Going the extra mile can't be a one-off—it has to be common practice, an attitude of the heart that's deeply ingrained in a company's modus operandi.

Many times in my professional career I have been personally struck by the importance of going the extra mile. Two experiences stand out:

One morning, back in my real estate days, I was talking on the phone to a very good client of mine, the president of a large financial institution. Usually a chatty, cheerful type of guy, he seemed surprisingly down in the mouth. During the course of our conversation, I discovered why: He mentioned that his son had just left for college, and he and his wife were finding it very lonely without him.

As a dad of six, I was troubled by what he said. All that day I thought about how I could help him feel better about the situation. So, on the way home, I stopped by the bookstore, found a book on strategies to deal with empty-nest syndrome, and sent it to him. A few days later he called me and, his voice full of gratitude, said that when he received the book it had brought tears to his eyes. It was a small gesture on my part, but the feeling of deep satisfaction I got from knowing that I'd helped this man was enormous. In the years that followed, he became my single most valuable customer and sent many referrals to my business.

Another example is one of the fondest memories of my real estate career. A client of mine, Lisa, was moving into her new home. As was my custom, I stopped by with pizzas and drinks for all her family members who were helping her move. Moving day is a big deal, and I always liked to personally be on hand to make sure everything was as it should be with the house, but when I arrived, there was no happy scene of celebration. Instead, Lisa was sitting on her front porch crying her eyes out. It turned out that her husband, Tom, had been called away on business and none of her family had been able to make it over to help her move in. She was completely overwhelmed—alone with a baby, a toddler, and a moving truck in her driveway. Immediately, I knew I had to help her out, but I was in a pickle because I had an appointment lined up. What was I going to do? Looking at her tearstained face, I knew there was only one option: I had to reschedule my appointment and stay to help this woman. I asked her what was most pressing . . . and that's how I found myself on my hands and knees in the nursery trying (and failing!) to put together a baby's crib! Let's just say my DIY skills will not be featured on HGTV any time soon. I called my office and asked for reinforcements, and we managed to get the baby's room in order and everything unloaded from the truck. I will never forget how incredibly grateful Lisa was for the help and how deeply satisfying it felt to go the extra mile to serve someone. By the way, Lisa was also a fountain of referrals through the years. And all those referrals had heard the story of that moving day . . . and the baby's crib.

Now, I don't recount these stories to blow my own trumpet. In fact, I don't think I did anything particularly special—no more than anyone else who puts their customers first would have. Technically, I may have been the one serving these people, but the incredible thing is that I think I was the one who benefited most. I learned an invaluable lesson from both experiences: Going the extra mile always feels good, and it pays well!

Go Above and Beyond

In every customer interaction, there's a basic level of performance— the business does what's required to meet the consumer's need and the transaction is completed. But only by consistently going above and beyond the basics will a business create customer loyalty—and more profit.

Luxury hotel group Four Seasons is expert at the "above-and-beyond" principle. Before guests arrive at a Four Seasons hotel, on file will be an individual cheat sheet detailing their preferred snacks, favorite flowers, and even which side of the bed they like to sleep on! No stone is left unturned, and nothing is left to chance in order to give each and every guest the experience of a lifetime. Staff—from management to front desk and beyond—are passionate about giving their customers exceptional care. Many luxury hotels offer helipads or top-of-the-line spas, but very few offer such minute attention to detail. Is it any wonder that the Four Seasons is a leader in the luxury hotel field?

The truth is, a business doesn't have to splash huge amounts of cash to show it cares. Even the smallest of gestures counts and can help to build relationships. Whether it's the grocery store employee who offers to carry heavy bags of groceries to a customer's car or the hair salon that loans a newly coiffed client an umbrella when it's raining, tiny gestures can create a strong and lasting impression—and even more so when they are unexpected.

Let me give you another example of how going above and beyond and doing the unexpected extras for your customers can make you exceptional.

Twenty-five years ago on our first wedding anniversary, Beverly and I walked into the Chart House in Oceanside, California, a beautiful seafood restaurant overlooking the marina, and that's where we first met Richard, our waiter. A twenty-year veteran of the business, Richard was very engaging. He set out to get to know us by asking questions, making recommendations on the menu, and ensuring we had everything we needed to enjoy our evening. He brought tremendous care and energy to his job—it was obvious this man loved what he did and was a master at it.

For the next twenty-five years, every time I would ask Bev where she'd like to celebrate a special occasion, she would say,

"Let's go see Richard!" We were so loyal to his service that, when the restaurant closed down and Richard moved thirty-odd miles away to another Chart House location, we went with him. Now don't get me wrong, his new place of employment is very nice and the food is very good, but the reason we go there is because Richard has made us feel valued for over a quarter of a century. We have a relationship with him that goes far beyond any transaction. Whenever we are asked for a restaurant referral, we always say, "Go to the Chart House and ask for Richard." It warms our hearts when the feedback we get is superb—because of Richard, many of our family members, friends, and coworkers have enjoyed wonderful occasions in his care.

It reminds me of what my mentor Jim Rohn once said: "One customer well taken care of could be more valuable than ten thousand dollars of advertising." How right he was!

Because Richard always made Beverly and me feel so special and well taken care of, it became almost impossible for us to celebrate our anniversary anywhere else. Richard gave something that many of us, as consumers, crave—a personalized experience. How did he do this? By always going above and beyond.

There are no traffic jams along the extra mile.
—ROGER STAUBACH

Give Something Extra

Throwing in a small product or service for free is an excellent way to reinforce a buying decision your customer just made. Everyone loves receiving something for nothing. I sure would have appreciated it if that Irish resort had made those bathing caps complimentary, for example! It would have been a small gesture on the hotel's part, but ultimately it would have meant that I wouldn't have canceled the remainder of our reservation and cost that establishment thousands of dollars in lost revenue—and thousands more in potential future business.

Businesses can be wary of giving free extras because of cost implications, but it's a strategy that doesn't have to incur huge cost. Psychologist Norbert Schwarz found that as little as ten cents can create reciprocity between two people. And for every cent you spend investing in your customers, you will reap multiples in return. Compare this to the income forever lost when you lose a customer.

Notice a Need

When you're interacting with customers, you must take the time to determine if they have an immediate need or challenge that you can help them address. Fixing a problem they're having may turn out to be the unexpected extra that makes their day. This is more than being kind and helpful (although these two attributes are, of course, very important!), it's watching to see if you can help your customers when they might not even know they need help. In general, people don't spend much time thinking about what their needs might be; and if they do, they may have difficulty expressing them to you. You must be on high alert and anticipate what your customers might want or need before they even know themselves, and that means drawing from your own previous experiences or stepping into their shoes and seeing the world through their eyes.

At the Four Seasons hotel in Paris, for example, an employee noticed that visitors were sometimes dazzled by the unexpectedly bright sun in the courtyard. Sunglasses of various styles are now kept on hand so that no guest need ever squint again! A small detail—but what a thoughtful touch of class.

Make It Right, Then Make It Better

When things go wrong, a business must not only apologize and rectify the situation—it must make the customer feel even better off than before. Say, for example, you purchase a faulty toaster. You take it back and get a replacement or a refund. Technically, the store has done right by you. But your experience could have been much better. If the store had given you that replacement or refund plus a voucher for a 10 percent discount off your next purchase for the inconvenience, you would have left with a spring in your step, feeling far happier and ready to come back and do business again. Studies have found that customers often switch allegiances, even when they're pretty satisfied with a product or service. They don't need an excuse to stop doing business with you, so give them a reason to remain loyal.

Take a Personal Interest

In a study from the *Journal of Applied Social Psychology,* researchers found that waiters could increase their tips by 23 percent by the simple act of returning to tables with a second set of mints. Can after-dinner mints perform miracles? No! But by giving people a second helping, waiters created the feeling of a personalized experience—and customers responded in a great way. The personal touch is vital in today's fast-paced world, when consumers often feel that the companies they do business with treat them more like numbers than individuals.

If you go to a restaurant and order a Caesar salad and you get a Caesar salad that tastes fine, then you got what you expected—there's nothing to be wowed about. But if you get a free drink with your salad, and your server was unusually attentive, then you are not just satisfied, you're impressed. Those personal touches may be small, but you'll remember them and tell others to eat at that restaurant. Likewise, if you have an unsatisfactory experience, you'll tell people to stay away.

No business can afford to be faceless. Whether in person or on social media, you must interact with and engage in your customers' needs in a genuine, timely, and authentic way. Get to know them and let them get to know you. At Buffini & Company, we have found that writing personal notes (something that used to be so much more common) is a highly effective way of connecting with customers. We send out tens of thousands of notes each year, which is one of the things that has contributed to the sense of personal connection our customers feel with our staff.

R.E.S.P.E.C.T.

If consumers feel disrespected, they will be disinclined to talk to you again, never mind give you repeat business! Whether it's during a run-of-the-mill interaction or when attempting to resolve a dispute or issue, showing your customer respect is paramount to creating a long-lasting relationship. If someone feels respected, they feel important and valued, which means they will be more inclined to share valuable feedback that could prevent similar issues from arising again.

Create Relationships

The only things that truly last in business are relationships. Products, markets, appetites, and tastes change, but if you keep tending to people, the relationships you have with them will endure. Historically, customers are loyal to the individuals in a business, not the business itself. And that relational dynamic still exists today. However, the world

> *Every great business is built on friendship.*
> —J. C. PENNEY

we live in now uses technology to drive efficiencies in all markets and businesses. If you provide the best value in terms of price, quality, or efficiency *and* you have a personal relationship, that's the best of both worlds. To create this relationship, you must treat your customers as kings and queens: Without them, your business simply won't last.

The Two-Way Street

Too often businesses undertake surveys and ask for customer feedback, but then do nothing with the information gathered. This just shows your customer that you don't value what they have to say. But if you tell your customers that communication is a two-way street—

that you want to hear from them—you are creating an environment that welcomes their suggestions to improve your product or service. In the process, you will strengthen their trust in and loyalty to your company. But remember: There's little point in asking customers for their honest feedback unless you act on it when you get it!

In the Loop

By the same token, for better or worse, it's imperative to keep customers informed about changes to your product or service. Customers don't like to be surprised—they can become very attached to the way things have always been done—so it's important to keep them in the loop. If you're planning to change something or you've added a service, made a mistake, or done something well, communicate it with your clients. This is the only way to create true transparency and trust.

Thanks a Million!

We all know how it feels to be taken for granted, so be sure not to let your customers feel that way. Always thank them for their business— let them know how much they are appreciated.

Put Your Customers' Needs First

Many businesses fail when it comes to the personalized customer experience. A business that focuses solely on what its competitors are doing to succeed only competes with what they, maybe wrongly, consider important. By stepping back and identifying your own customers' fundamental needs, however, you can almost eliminate the need to battle with competitors.

The goal of creating and delivering value for customers should be at the heart of every company's manifesto. It's a simple, yet highly effective, strategy: Put your customers' needs first, give them consistent and exceptional value, and your business will reap the rewards.

CHALLENGE 9: LEVERAGE THE RUN/REST CYCLE

"Go hard or go home" is a battle cry heard on sports fields around the world, a rousing slogan used to remind players that victory can often require blood, sweat, and tears. It's well known that achieving success and reaching our goals means being relentless in approach and "going hard" by bringing energy, passion, and all-in commitment to everything we do. But what's less spoken of is the importance of "resting hard" too.

These days many of us are in a constant state of high-anxiety motion. We have a million things on our to-do list and never enough hours in the day. Taking time to rest and renew isn't something we respect or prioritize. But we should!

The concept of maximizing performance by alternating periods of activity with periods of rest was first championed by Flavius Philostratus (A.D. 170–ca. 245), who composed training manuals for Greek athletes. Russian sports scientists revived the concept in the 1960s and applied it with incredible success to that country's Olympic athletes. Today, "work-rest" ratios lie at the heart of periodization, a training method used by elite athletes throughout the world. If it's good enough for Olympic athletes, then it has to be good enough for us too! Top athletes don't go straight from one tough race to another. They understand that if they don't regularly renew their energy their performance will suffer, so they build planned recovery periods into their training schedules. They train hard, run hard, and then they rest hard before they start again. This is how they maintain peak performance. Taking these breaks means they can come back to their next training cycle raring to go and with renewed vigor and hunger. On the other hand, runners who go from one race to another, never taking time out in between, eventually lose the will to compete altogether.

Periods of high-intensity performance, followed by some R&R time, are the key to long-term success.

In *The Power of Full Engagement*, authors Jim Loehr and Tony Schwartz said the ability to rest and recover from intense activity is the key to high performance. According to them, in order to maintain a powerful pulse in our lives we must all learn how to rhythmically spend and renew energy by utilizing the work-rest ratio.

Here's the thing—we're not machines. We are designed to intermittently expend and recover energy. The most fundamental thing we do is breathe in and out—you can't do just one. We have brain waves that have high and low frequency. Our muscles are meant to contract *and* relax. We need to shift between activity and rest. Regular renewal and recovery make us healthier, happier, and able to perform better. It's also when growth occurs.

We must ennoble the idea of renewal and recovery, and we need to treat our bodies and minds with care and respect or we will burn out. If we expect ourselves to consistently perform at top capacity, we must schedule regular periods to recuperate and recharge. If we don't, the grind of always running will eventually wear us down. I'm not saying we need to turn into couch potatoes, with the remote in one hand and chips in the other! Science has shown this to be the worst sort of recovery there is. Good, restorative recovery can take many forms—spending time with family and friends, going on vacation, or pursuing hobbies that we're passionate about.

Over the years, I have found different ways to recharge. I've developed daily disciplines of prayer, exercising, and resting. During my working day, my assistant comes to get me every ninety minutes to remind me to have a quiet moment or two. I take Beverly on a date night once a week, and once a quarter, I go on a trip with my family. The very anticipation of these varied activities is motivating. They not only refresh and revitalize me; they also feed into my work in unexpected ways. Often, if I'm stuck on some issue, I take a break and the solution comes to me immediately after. Sometimes it's difficult to force myself to get off that wheel and take a breath. But I know that when I do, I will benefit and my work will too. Doing something you find fun and stimulating means you come back to your duties with more energy and zeal than ever. By stepping away and focusing on something else for a while, you can rediscover the desire, motivation, and passion that drive you to excel in the workplace . . . and you can then challenge yourself to perform even better than before.

So I advise you to go as hard and as fast as you can, then take time to recuperate and introduce some fun into your life before you get back on the attack again. Your business will reap phenomenal rewards, and so will you.

CHAPTER TWENTY-ONE

How to Cultivate a Heartfelt Spirit of Gratitude

For the past twenty years, I've had the privilege of teaching and training more than three million people all over the world how to live the American Dream. I've heard many stories of transformation and triumph, and I've met countless people, many of them immigrants who, like me, came to this country with nothing and went on to build a fortune and a family. The most common thread among them all? Gratitude.

It's been scientifically proven that an attitude of gratitude benefits your physical and mental health, your relationships, your sleep patterns, your self-esteem, and your resilience. As the old saying goes, "If you've forgotten the language of gratitude, you'll never be on speaking terms with happiness."

Successful immigrants are naturally grateful for the countless opportunities this country gives them. A deep and pervading sense of gratitude colors their attitude toward everything, and that gives them an edge in business and in life. To get that same edge, we should focus on embracing that very same mind-set. We all have the ability to jump-start the upward spiral of well-being that is triggered by outward expressions of gratitude. Deliberately cultivating gratitude and, as a result, increasing happiness costs nothing, and it doesn't take much time. Here's how:

CHALLENGE 10: APPRECIATE THOSE CLOSEST TO YOU

It's nine o'clock on a Friday evening and I'm looking at the faces of my six children. They're preparing to dig into enormous cups of frozen yogurt, smothered with mountains of delicious toppings that defy the laws of physics! Before they take a bite, I raise my own spoon in the air and say the refrain they've heard since they were infants.

Gratitude: The quality of being thankful; readiness to show appreciation for and to return kindness.
—*OXFORD ENGLISH DICTIONARY*

"It's a good life, kids!"

"It's a good life, Dad," they all beam back, before proceeding to demolish their desserts.

Don't you love small moments of joy like that—when you realize how blessed you are and how grateful you should be to share everyday pleasures with the people closest to you? Sadly, in today's world, we can forget to cherish and celebrate simple, precious moments spent with our family and friends. Thanks to the Hollywood ideal of perfection that we're constantly (and often subliminally) subjected to, many of us are in pursuit of unrealistic emotional highs, mountain-top experiences, and a sense that everything should always be going our way. It's really no surprise that we begin to feel that anything less just isn't good enough: From reality TV shows that celebrate wealth and acquisition above all else, to social media posts that only portray the heavily edited show-reel of other people's lives, we're inundated with the idea that perfection is not only standard but required. As a result, it's easy to become dissatisfied with our circumstances and miss out on the fact that the life we're living, which admittedly may need improvements or enhancements, is inherently good.

In Freedom Hall in Philadelphia, for example, when people line up to see the famous Liberty Bell, they focus on the crack. Yet the crack represents just a tiny percentage of the circumference of the entire bell. When it comes to our lives, we have a tendency to repeat the same mistake. When we think of our health and well-being, we see the blemishes, the wrinkles, and the spare tire, but rarely take inventory of how well our bodies are functioning. When we focus on our finances, we worry about our bills and obligations, but never take time to be truly thankful for all that we have. In our relationships, we ruminate on the hurts and disappointments, instead of reveling in the beauty of our strong and healthy connections. In business, we fret about the sales goal missed, the one unhappy client, or the staff member who just left. It's no wonder so many people suffer with a relentless and gnawing sense of unease and unhappiness.

The good news is that we can learn to change our thought processes, adapt our patterns of behavior, and embrace an "attitude of gratitude." Like the most successful immigrants, however, we must first acknowledge and accept that life has its ups and downs. By focusing on our blessings instead of on what we lack or want, we can experience much more of what's good in life. Gratitude and entitlement cannot coexist. We must concentrate on being thankful for the small things—for they are actually the big things.

By appreciating those closest to you—family, friends, and work colleagues—you are taking one step closer to living a contented, successful life. Gratitude transforms everything in your life, and it starts with small gestures to those in your immediate circle. My greatest achievement is the knowledge that Beverly and I have raised six very grounded

> *The more you praise and celebrate your life, the more there is in life to celebrate.*
> —OPRAH WINFREY

and grateful children. They know how blessed we are and don't take it for granted, but we regularly remind them just how good life is (in all its ups and downs). We also strive to practice what we preach. As well as showing the kids the joyful value of being thankful for everyday miracles, we make sure to consistently thank them for sharing with one another and with friends, for doing their chores, and for communicating with others in a mannerly and respectful way. We want them to know that we appreciate their efforts too. The beauty of this approach is that the well of gratitude just keeps on filling up!

CHALLENGE 11: CATCH PEOPLE DOING SOMETHING RIGHT

It's easy to find things to criticize in this world. In fact, if we're not careful, we can find ourselves noticing *only* what others do wrong! We need to do a 180 and start noticing when people do things right!

For example, it's a core parenting principle that instead of scolding children when they misbehave, you should try to catch them doing well and praise them for it instead. It's far healthier, more encouraging, and motivating for children to get positive feedback instead of negative criticism. Not only does it foster stronger parent-child relationships, it results in positive growth patterns, increased self-esteem, and better behavior.

In business, the same basic principle applies. For example, it's no good insisting your team express gratitude to customers if you don't do the same! A 2014 survey by Boston Consulting Group found that workers valued appreciation for their work higher than career development or even salary! It's a basic human need to feel valued. If you work to actively notice when someone does something right and thank them for it, instead of nitpicking when they do something wrong, it will be hugely beneficial to all the relationships in your life.

But it's not enough to just say thanks—you have to really and truly mean it! People can tell when a thank-you isn't sincere and, ironically, it can have the opposite effect of the one you're hoping to achieve.

All too often, we just mutter a distracted thank-you to people when they go out of their way to help us—the clerk at the checkout, the waitress in the diner, or the barista in the coffeehouse. Does this make the other person feel appreciated or valued? No! It makes them feel like an afterthought or an obligation. Saying thank you just to "tick a box" isn't enough. You must really connect with the person you're thanking. If that means putting down your phone for five seconds and looking the other person in the eye when you speak, or taking out a pen and paper to compose a genuine and heartfelt letter of thanks, even when you can think of a million other things you could do, just do it!

Likewise, when it comes to your internal monologue, it's vital to really embrace gratitude as an attitude, with body, mind, and spirit.

> *Feeling gratitude and not expressing it is like wrapping a present and not giving it.*
> —WILLIAM ARTHUR WARD

Catch yourself doing something right and give yourself a pat on the back! This can take some getting used to—it can be difficult to learn to focus on the positive and good—but it gets easier and more automatic with practice. Waiting for gratitude in your heart to magically occur without investing any effort doesn't work. Even if you're not entirely satisfied with your life as it is today, you can still be grateful in your attitude. It's like training yourself to stand up straight. If you improve your posture, something in you shifts—you become more self-confident and energetic. When you express gratitude, your mind-set shifts and you experience all the many benefits.

You can actually rewire yourself to see good in the world. To train your brain, simply focus on positive things for three minutes every day. You can do this by writing in a journal, meditating, or sharing with someone what it is you're most grateful for. It can be anything from a beautiful sunrise, to a fresh, hot cup of coffee or a vacant parking spot in a jam-packed lot! Noticing things for which you're grateful very quickly attunes the brain to positivity.

CHALLENGE 12: BRUSH YOUR TEETH AND WRITE YOUR NOTES

I remember the first time I was introduced to the phenomenal power of the thank-you note. It was 1992 and President George Bush Senior was being interviewed about his career as congressman, director of the CIA, vice president, and president. The interviewer asked a simple question: "What's the one thing you've done in your life to make you so successful?"

The president's response was so simple and profound it stopped me dead in my tracks. He said that for the previous twenty-five years he had written at least ten personal notes a day to people he'd recently met, those who came to mind, or correspondents who had written to him. Now, at the time of this interview, I was living in a little "white house" myself, and I believe that when people at the top of the ladder give you clues on success, it's a good idea to take heed. And so I did. I sat and wrote my first note. Twenty-five years later, I'm still writing them!

In fact, for the past quarter century I have sent several thousand notes a year. I'm a prolific note writer to my clients, staff, family, and friends. I firmly believe that the cumulative effect of all that goodwill over time has been one of the key ingredients of my success.

Personal notes expressing gratitude have incredible power. When people open their mail, a personal note is always the first thing they read. After all, it stands out among all the junk mail and bills! And in this high-tech, social media–driven world, I find personal notes are even more powerful and better received than ever before. I've often saved a meaningful note or letter that someone has written to me, and I know I'm not alone.

My whole family writes personal notes of thanks to people who have helped or inspired them. I remember that my daughter Anna, after becoming an international dressage champion, once wrote a note to a trainer, saying how grateful she was for her assistance and guidance. The trainer was thrilled to receive this letter, but she was also shocked. "Brian," she said, "no one has ever written me a thank-you note before! I'll never forget this letter."

This is the sort of positive impression that a simple thank-you note can have on someone. It takes just minutes to compose, but the impact can last many years. Inside the walls of Buffini & Company we even have our very own card store, where staff can simply walk in and pick a card for free for any occasion. You can't put a price on the goodwill that departs our mailroom in thousands of personal notes and cards each week. We remind our clients every day that it's important to be intentional about expressing their gratitude toward their customers. Make acknowledging and thanking people part of your daily routine.

> *As we express our gratitude, we must never forget that the highest appreciation is not to utter words, but to live by them.*
> —JOHN F. KENNEDY

Just like brushing your teeth or writing tomorrow's to-do list, it will become automatic. Over time, if you don't do it, it will feel like something's wrong—as if you're walking around with bad breath!

I have hundreds of stories I could share on the power of expressing gratitude through a note. Here are just a couple:

It was Christmas Eve, 1999. As we tucked our four kids into bed, the phone rang. A lady introduced herself: "You don't know me," she said, "but years ago you sold my father's house." She mentioned his name, but nothing rang a bell. That late on Christmas Eve my mind was far away from a house that had sold many years before. "I'm sorry," I admitted, "I'm drawing a blank on your dad."

She mentioned the street where he had lived and suddenly it all came flooding back. In a flash, I remembered the day I first met her father. He had called me shortly after becoming a widower. His beloved wife of forty-six years had passed away six months before and he was a heartbroken man, struggling to carry on without her. His daughter wanted him to move back east and live with her—but he was unsure what to do.

The day I met him, I had a full schedule of appointments, but after speaking with him for a short while I canceled everything to spend more time with him. In truth, we barely got around to talking about business or putting his home on the market—instead, we sat and he told me his life story. When I got back to the office, I wrote him a heartfelt letter telling him how much I respected him as a devoted husband and father. I wrote that I hoped to be privileged enough to be married for forty-six years, and if I lost my wife I would be every bit as heartbroken as he was.

The reason his daughter was calling me on Christmas Eve was to let me know that he had passed away recently, and when they went to read from his personal Bible at his eulogy, they found that the letter I had written him had served as a bookmark for his daily readings. It had been ten years since I had sold that home. And in one way or another, he had read or looked at that letter every day since. You just never know what a word of gratitude or appreciation will do for the recipient.

The second story I want to tell you is about the legendary astronaut Neil Armstrong. For many years, I wanted Mr. Armstrong to be a guest speaker at our annual MasterMind Summit®. I wrote to him often, asking him to come and telling him how grateful I was for his service to this great country. The reply was always the same—he was retired. But I persisted . . . for a long time. Eventually, he wrote back to ask if I was going to keep writing to him until he agreed to come out of retirement! My answer was, of course . . . yes! This is how I eventually had the very great privilege of interviewing Mr. Armstrong in front of a riveted audience. To hear this incredible human being recall his journey to the moon remains one of the highlights of my career—and a testament to the power of the personal note!

So it's fair to say that gratitude is good for business. But better than that, it's good for you, it's a great way to live, and it's the foundation for living the good life.

CHAPTER TWENTY-TWO

How to Acquire a Boldness to Invest

When people think about investing, they often feel intimidated. "I don't have the money, resources, or wherewithal to invest," they say. "I'm no Warren Buffett!" However, when I refer to a boldness to invest, I'm not talking about stocks and shares in a company. I'm talking about investing in growth for your future. I'm not saying to think like an investment guru—I want you to think like a farmer.

Farming is one of the principal occupations back in my home country of Ireland. This small island is world-renowned for its delicious beef, creamy dairy products, and wholesome vegetables. Irish farmers punch above their weight on the world stage because they are so focused on quality and high standards.

I've always believed that a farming philosophy is a good analogy for life. If you want your crops to flourish, you have to put in the groundwork. You must clear the weeds, prepare the soil for planting, and then tend to the seeds carefully so they'll grow. If you don't, then what you've planted won't produce a crop. If you want your cows to produce the finest milk, you must care for them and feed them the sweetest grass. The same is true of us and our lives: If we want to thrive, we must tend to our needs with the same planning and thought that the farmer invests in his livestock and land. Only then will we reap the greatest rewards for our labor.

Throughout this book, I have asked you to think about your own history. If any of us were to go far enough back in our ancestral lineage, at some point in time we would find somebody who tilled the land and worked with animals. That's who I want you to identify with. Think about what it took for

> *Don't judge each day by the harvest you reap, but by the seeds that you plant.*
> —ROBERT LOUIS STEVENSON

him to survive and begin emulating the same qualities. Then you will discover how to invest boldly and leverage this aspect of the Emigrant Edge.

CHALLENGE 13: SOW THE SEEDS OF SELF-DEVELOPMENT

We talk a lot about self-development here at Buffini & Company. It's so important that we've made committing to personal growth one of our core values as a business. Why do we place so much emphasis on it? It's simple: We know that a commitment to continuous growth and learning keeps our skills sharp, allows us to serve our clients better, and is essential to our lasting success.

One of my favorite quotes is: "Amateurs practice until they get it right; professionals practice until they can't get it wrong." Even when you're at the top of your game, it's important to keep sharpening your skills through practice and never-ending self-improvement.

Over the years, we've had many guests speak at our live events—and time and time again their message shores up the philosophy that if you want to take your business to the next level, you must adopt a mind-set for growth and a commitment to personal development.

Now this isn't always easy. Many small business owners want to grow personally, but they genuinely believe they simply don't have the time to invest in their own personal development. They work long and brutal hours, rarely taking a break to rest or rejuvenate. In an effort to keep ahead of the game, they don't create boundaries: Their professional life bleeds into their home and leisure time. They drift into a pattern of work that consumes more and more time, and they rationalize away the dreams of having a balanced, fulfilled life and achieving personal growth. They're frustrated, anxious, overworked, and overwhelmed. They're also sleep-deprived, exhausted, and so focused on looking after their business that they don't care for their minds, bodies, or spirits. They keep battling through by telling themselves that things will change tomorrow. All the while, the stress builds inside, like in a pressure cooker.

It's a scientific fact that stress can be deadly. According to a 2015 working paper from Harvard and Stanford business schools, health problems stemming from job stress, like hypertension, cardiovascular disease, and decreased mental health, can lead to fatal conditions that result in the deaths of about 120,000 people each year. This makes work-related stressors even deadlier than diseases such as diabetes or Alzheimer's. That's a shocking report. Think about it: For *up to 120,000 people every year,* the tomorrow they dream of simply never comes.

When I was a young man, I believed that I could achieve both the financial freedom I wanted and the fullness of life I craved in harmony with each other. Despite my best intentions, however, as my business grew there were too many evenings I came home late for dinner, too many afternoons spent negotiating on a cell phone at my kids' soccer games, and too many hours being preoccupied or exhausted when I could have been pursuing other passions.

I was on the brink of burnout before I realized I was in danger of derailing the dreams I had when I first came to America. Instead of having the harmonious existence that I craved, I was letting my business run my life. I was all in professionally, but other aspects of my life were suffering because I had what I call an either/or mind-set. It was one or the other—my job or my family.

I know that many of you reading this right now are experiencing this same problem. Even though you know intellectually that it's possible to grow and achieve success, you are struggling with some roadblocks in your path that prevent you from sowing those seeds of self-development:

Four Roadblocks to Self-Development

1. Fear

Many of us are afraid of change. It's the classic fear of the unknown. We stay in situations, jobs, or relationships that are no good for us. We keep clinging to what we know, even when it's clear that change is needed for circumstances to improve.

We might also fear being mocked or ridiculed. If we try to do things differently, will people judge us or laugh at our efforts? This sort of response is often a deep-rooted emotional throwback to our childhood, when standing out wasn't a good thing, and to be part of the crowd was all that mattered.

And last, but certainly not least, there's the fear of failure. If we don't try, then we're guaranteed that we won't fail. We'll stay safe as we are—or at least we think we will. Fear of failure stops many people from ever realizing their full potential. But staying where you are is a false sense of security—an illusion. As Eleanor Roosevelt said, "You gain strength, courage and confidence by every experience in which you really stop to look fear in the face. . . . You must do the thing you think you cannot do."

2. Lack of Discipline and Motivation

Changing how we operate and trying new things requires discipline and motivation. It's not easy to summon up extra energy when you're already exhausted by the load you're carrying. Change is often difficult and overwhelming, and slipping back into old habits is easy. That's why a system is so important.

Having grandiose plans to make change is all well and good, but unless you have a workable system in place to help and support you, you will never succeed. You have to be accountable to yourself—not only to keep on track and motivated, but to give yourself encouragement and show yourself how far you've really come. For any growth plan to truly work, it must be backed by a well-thought-through and implemented system. Get yourself a *system*, and you will *Save Yourself Time Energy and Money!*

3. No Support

The journey to change can be a lonely one . . . but only if you let it. No one expects you to go it alone. Why travel the path of change on your own when you can walk with an ally by your side to support and guide you? Lean on your coaches and mentors. Read everything you can. Follow the tracks your heroes have left for you. As I've already said, there's a wealth of resources out there just waiting for you to discover.

4. Lack of Self-Awareness

If you don't know what you want to change or where you should start, it can be easier just to stay where you are. But, the truth is, you're not going to become all you can be by standing still. As Lou Holtz says, you have to "get in motion." Only by conscious effort will your life improve. Do an audit of your own life: Assess and evaluate how you live and work. What are the skills that you can develop, the habits you can improve, or the attitudes that can be enhanced? Discover who you are and who you want to be. Invest in yourself. If you don't, then who will? Remember: The formula for achievement is composed of mind-set, motivation, and methodologies. A cord of three strands has immense strength and is not easily broken!

Three Reasons to Commit to Self-Development

1. *You Will Find Your Purpose*

When you commit to growth, you open the door to ongoing learning—both about your career or industry and about yourself. Not only does this help you find your true purpose, if you haven't already, it also helps refine it. You'll be happier, work more effectively, and offer your best self to your clients and loved ones.

2. *You Will Get Inspired*

Hearing and learning from the stories of others can motivate you to improve your life and business and help you to stay on track to reach your goals, especially when challenges arise. Choosing a daily quote to think about is a great way to stay inspired. If you need ideas, download our free ebook, *25 Motivational Quotes to Inspire Your Success*, available at www.buffiniandcompany.com.

3. You Will Start Living the Life You Want to Live

Many people feel stuck in a rut in their careers and lives. Personal growth and development provide the tools you need to rise above your circumstances and realize your full potential.

The change starts with a shift in your way of thinking. You must challenge the negatives you believe about yourself that hold you back and seize the opportunities that come your way every day.

My mentor Jim Rohn always counseled people to ponder these four questions for a successful life:

- Why?

- Why not?

- Why not you?

- Why not now?

You have what it takes to do what you want. All you need is the mind-set, the methodologies, and the motivation. The right mind-set will give you direction, the methodologies will sustain you, and the motivation will be your driving force to success. Remember: Even the smallest of seeds can yield the most amazing results. Consider the parable of the mustard seed—the tiniest of all seeds. When it grew, it became larger than all the other plants, putting out great branches so that birds of the sky could lodge under its

> *People often say motivation doesn't last. Well, neither does bathing. That's why we recommend it daily.*
> —ZIG ZIGLAR

shadow. When it comes to self-development, even the smallest steps toward growth can have an enormous impact. Over time, you will reap what you sow.

CHALLENGE 14: FEED THE GOLDEN GOOSE

In *The 7 Habits of Highly Effective People,* Stephen R. Covey explains a principle called "P/PC Balance." This principle can be understood by thinking of Aesop's fable, "The Goose and the Golden Egg." In this story, a farmer discovers that his goose has laid a golden egg. He can't believe it. Thinking it must be some kind of trick, he takes the egg to be appraised and discovers that it's solid gold! He has won the lottery. The next day, the goose does it again, and the day after that too. The farmer is overjoyed—he is wealthy beyond his wildest dreams!

But soon the farmer begins to get impatient with the goose. He's not satisfied with just one egg a day—he gets greedy and wants more. He decides to kill the goose and get all the eggs inside. But when he does, he finds there are no more eggs. Now the goose is dead—and there's no way of getting any more. He has destroyed his own good fortune.

What this story demonstrates is that true effectiveness is the result of two things: 1) the product (the golden egg) and 2) the ability to produce or the asset that produces (the goose). One relies on the other. In life, if you only focus on your golden eggs and neglect your goose, you will be in trouble. Likewise, if you only focus on your goose with no regard for your golden eggs, in a short time you won't have the ability to feed either yourself or the goose.

The two go hand in hand; effectiveness can only be achieved when we follow Covey's "P/PC Balance." The P stands for the *Production* of the desired results: the golden eggs. The PC stands for the *Production Capability*: the ability or asset that produces the golden eggs.

As an immigrant to this country, I have always been very aware of protecting the assets I have at my disposal. I have never taken any of them for granted because I came from nothing and I was aware that I could end up with nothing again if I wasn't careful. My advice to you is to protect the assets in your life.

We all have three kinds of assets: tangible, financial, and human.

A *tangible asset* could be your car or your house. If you don't change the oil in your car on a regular basis, for example, then the engine will be damaged and the car will devalue. If you don't caulk the windows on your house, they will leak.

A *financial asset* could be your savings. We live in a consumer-driven society and temptation to spend is everywhere. But dipping into your savings without caution will diminish your kids' college fund or your retirement fund. Likewise, in business, you must protect your company's financial assets—such as bank deposits, bonds, or stocks—or pay the consequences.

A *human asset* is the relationship you have with family, friends, staff, or customers. If you take them for granted, the relationship (and your business) will suffer badly.

CHALLENGE 15: TEND TO THE TREE

When you're making a lot of effort to grow, it can be very frustrating when you see no evidence that you're succeeding. You can be tempted to give up—after all, if you're getting nowhere, what's the point of trying so hard? But, sometimes, not everything is as it seems. Not all progress is visible—it can happen out of sight too. For example, when I'm feeling frustrated that I'm not getting where I want to go as fast as I'd like, I think about the Chinese bamboo tree.

The bamboo tree is one of the strongest, most resilient, and useful trees known to man. And it's unlike other trees. Instead of sprouting quickly, it stays under the ground for a very long time after it's planted. In fact, in the first year, there is zero visible growth. Same in the second, the third, and even the fourth year! It's only in the fifth year that shoots begin to appear. Then something incredible happens. Within six weeks of sprouting, the bamboo tree can grow to be ninety feet tall, seemingly out of nowhere! But the question is, did that bamboo tree grow overnight or over five years?

If you think about it, the bamboo tree has a lot in common with success and our perception of it. We can often look at others and wonder how they got to where they are so quickly. But just like the bamboo tree, their so-called overnight success was actually the result of years of unseen work.

Even when a bamboo tree is hidden underground, there is a lot of activity below the surface—roots are establishing themselves deep down into the earth. To the naked eye, the tree is getting nowhere fast, but just because you can't see something doesn't mean that progress isn't being made. It is the same with success. The

> *The warrior, like bamboo,*
> *is ever ready for action.*
> —ANONYMOUS

work behind the scenes can be invisible, but it can eventually result in phenomenal growth.

The truth is, you're not always going to grow the way you expect to. Life just isn't that straightforward. That's why it's important to be steadfast and persistent, even when you're not seeing results. The progress may not be as fast as you'd like, but developing your roots will make you stronger in the long run. So next time you think you're getting nowhere fast, think of that bamboo tree and keep being faithful with the little things. They will get you the results you want eventually.

CHAPTER TWENTY-THREE

How to Develop a Commitment to Delay Gratification

Most of us are naturally wired to want to do what is fun and easy in life. That's why we treat ourselves to a little retail therapy, even though we know it will bust our budget. It's why we vow to eat healthy and improve our diet, but then stop for takeout on the way home from work. It's why we promise to go for a run, but end up on the sofa watching TV instead. We might think all of this is pretty harmless behavior, but the opposite is true: this inability to delay gratification is one of the main causes of economic and personal failure in life.

Delayed gratification is not some extraordinary test of willpower for its own sake—it's the discipline required to ultimately have your goals and dreams come to pass. You can live the good life later if you're willing to say no to a few things now. Of course, saying no doesn't come naturally. Denying yourself pleasure is hard. But if you always say yes to life's shortcuts, then you never get the big payoff down the road. And if you don't condition and train yourself to be disciplined, you're on the road to ruin.

CHALLENGE 16: LEARN TO SAY NO WITH A SMILE

We often know what we need to do to improve our lives. That's why we make plans to change our habits and vow to do better. But then we're confronted with a decision or a choice that could get us off course, and our mettle is put to the test. We know the right thing to do, but we do the opposite. Sometimes this is because of a lack of willpower, say, for example, when we use an almost maxed-out credit card to shop online for things we don't need or we overeat because we're bored. Other times, however, we make poor choices and decisions because we want to be well thought of by those who put temptation in our path (often without even realizing it); our people-pleasing impulse undermines the power of delayed gratification.

> *The ability to discipline yourself to delay gratification in the short term in order to enjoy greater rewards in the long term is the indispensable prerequisite for success.*
> —BRIAN TRACY

If you're going to benefit from the principle of delayed gratification, then you're going to have to be cured of the "disease to please." I used to suffer from this "disease" myself. I've worked on it, but I still like to be engaging and please people—after all, I come from a country that is world-famous for its friendly and hospitable nature. The truth of the matter is, most of us like to be liked. However, what I've discovered is that it's more important to be respected first and liked second.

When it comes to delayed gratification, the first person you need to respect is *you*. The definition of self-control is the ability to control your emotions in the face of temptations and impulses. If you want to unleash the power of delayed gratification and make it work for you, you can't be a people-pleaser and you can't forever give in to pleasing yourself. It's not respectful of yourself to give in to the easy option when you know it's not a wise choice. That sends a subliminal message to your subconscious that you're not worth the effort and willpower.

Stanford University psychologist Kelly McGonigal defines willpower as "the ability to do what matters most, even when it's difficult or when some part of you doesn't want to." She says we all have two conflicting selves. There's a part of us that thinks about the long-term picture and what it would look like once we achieve our goals. But there's another part of us that has a completely different agenda. This part wants to max out on pleasure and avoid those messy, irritating emotions like stress, pain, and discomfort that come with the work involved in meeting our goals. The decisions and choices that require willpower set those two competing selves against each other in a fierce battle. Willpower is the ability to stand firm with the part of you that prioritizes long-term goals—it's the part that will tolerate the short-term pain and discomfort often required to get the results you want. The problem, of course, is that it's extremely challenging to listen or submit to that part of you! But if you concentrate on respecting yourself first, accessing that part of you gets easier.

Just so you know, even when I am at my most disciplined, there are still parts of me that rebel! When I set goals to get fit and healthy, I still like a cup of Irish tea with a chocolate cookie. It's okay to reward yourself now and again—we're all human. But if you really want to reach your goals, you're going to have to apply the principle of delayed gratification at some point.

One of the best ways I've found to keep myself in check when I'm tempted to stray off track is to just say no, then smile. It's very simple but extremely effective because people don't take offense and you stay in control. Stop reading this now and practice. I mean it! Say the words "No, thank you," with a big smile afterward. Do it again—say the word *no* and have a big chuckle afterward. Once you start, it gets easier. So when temptation strikes, say no with a smile and keep your eyes on the prize.

CHALLENGE 17: SWIM AGAINST THE STREAM

Remember when you were in high school and all you wanted to do was blend into the crowd? At that age, fitting in with your peers was *everything*. That mind-set is understandable when you're young, but there comes a point later in adult life when you have to go your own way. As the old saying goes, "Don't follow the crowd, they don't know where they're going!"

Do you honestly believe that everyone around you is happy? If that's so, then why does one out of every eight Americans take antidepressants? Do you think that everyone is healthy? If that's the case, then why are more that 40 percent of Americans considered obese? What about prosperity? Is everybody rich and successful? I don't think so.

Now that's not to put anybody down or to say that people can't improve. If the principles of the Emigrant Edge outlined in this book are applied, anyone can go from where they are to where they want to be—and, for most people, that means a better place of personal fulfillment, health, and wealth. But if you want to get to a better place in life, you can't just follow the masses. You have to be countercultural. Let me give you a financial example of what I mean.

If you go to your local department store at Christmastime to buy a gift for somebody, you'll probably be offered a department store credit card. "If you activate and use the card today, you'll get a ten percent discount on your entire purchase!" That's what you'll hear. Now that may sound like a great deal, but the store is not giving you that card so you'll save money. The truth is, they want you to be on their finance plan.

Since I came to America, I've said no to every department store card I've ever been offered. Saying no means I've gone against the flow of most people. I've stood out. The clerks behind the counter are often shocked. "But, sir," they say, "you could save so much money!"

And yes, because I'm spending a lot of money in some of these circumstances, it's true I could save some. I could even pay off the card every month on time and in full. But I still say no. I'm the same way when it comes to paying ATM charges at the bank. I always carry around enough cash that I don't run out. And I'm the same when it comes to vacations—I won't go on one unless it's paid for beforehand.

If you want to be financially set, you must be countercultural. But this mind-set doesn't only apply to your financial situation. If you want to live a healthier lifestyle, for example, you've got to think and act counterculturally. When eating out, you can't automatically go for the sugary, fatty foods that others in your party might choose without even thinking about it—you've got to pick alternatives that fit within your healthy way of eating. Your choices must be intentional.

In every area of your life, if you always swim along with the current without knowing which direction you're going, you won't end up in a healthy place. The good news is, when you swim against the stream you develop muscles, you build strength, and you become healthier and stronger than ever. It's not always easy to go against the tide at the moment you're doing it, but over time it gets easier and, eventually, it will help lead you to success.

CHALLENGE 18: STAY IN SEQUENCE

When I was a boy I would rush from one place to another, always impatient to get to where I wanted to go. My mother used to say to me, "Don't put the cart before the horse!" By this she meant that I needed to be patient and do things in the right sequence if I wanted to succeed.

Everyday life is filled with events that move in a sequential or logical order. A child develops first by crawling, then progresses to walking, then running. Students first go to preschool, then elementary school, middle school, high school, and college. Couples advance from dating, to engagement, to marriage.

When it comes to financial success, the concept of sequence is one of the most important lessons I've ever learned. First identified by my mentor Zig Ziglar, the sequence of financial prosperity follows a natural progression: Survival, Stability, Success, and Significance.

This progression is like the metamorphosis of a caterpillar into a butterfly. In order for a caterpillar to transform, it must follow precise steps in a defined order. A caterpillar doesn't grow its wings overnight. Nature remains true to its design and there's no hurrying the process. The struggle the caterpillar must make in the darkness of its cocoon is vital to its transformation. Before it can achieve the ultimate freedom of flight, it must fight to release itself from the confinement of its chrysalis.

Each stage of your own financial sequence has a purpose and importance too. None of it should be hurried or done out of order. And while it won't be easy to change poor spending habits that have become ingrained, with discipline and incremental steps you can sever the monetary bonds that have stopped you from reaching your financial potential. If you want to progress through the sequence of success, you'll have to focus on each step. To get to the next level, keep your focus small.

Survival

When you're in survival mode, you can feel as if you've reached rock bottom. Your expenses and your debts are crushing you because your income is drastically inadequate to meet your financial obligations. Bills go unpaid, credit cards are maxed out, and savings are nonexistent. In this situation, people can often feel totally helpless because they see no way out. The good news is there's nowhere to go but up—as long as you start taking steps in the right direction.

Incrementally Increase Your Income

The biggest mistake you can make when your finances are in crisis is to chase some radical idea that promises to return a huge amount of money in a short amount of time. Now, this scenario is possible, but the fact remains that the most significant success follows an incremental path of growth that takes time.

Imagine a minor league baseball player trying to make a major league team—the difference between the two is the difference between making thousands or millions. Some rookies attempt to increase their score by going up to bat and trying to hit a home run every time. But what they really need to do is focus on getting one hit. A player who hits .250 risks losing his job, but a player who hits .300 is a superstar. The difference is just five extra hits every 100 times at bat. By focusing on getting just one hit at a time, a rookie can make small, incremental adjustments and improvements that pay big dividends in the end—it's the same for your financial situation. It might be the one small decision to go for coffee three times a week instead of seven, or to take a brown bag lunch to work instead of eating out, but all these small decisions can take your minor league finances to the major league.

Keep Your Cash Liquid

My dad used to say, "When you're on top of the mountain, throw a little dirt in the valley—it'll break your fall."

The dirt in the valley is an amount of cash you keep in reserve in case of emergency. Ideally, you should keep building your reserve until you have a cash cushion that will cover your home expenses for six months, but that thought can be overwhelming. So apply the incremental method by focusing on saving enough for one month, then three, then six . . . and keep going! There is tremendous peace and freedom that comes with having an emergency fund like this.

Institute a Spending Freeze at Home

A common mistake that people make when trying to correct their financial shape is to remove just one or two major items from their budget. This can help, but often it's the cumulative effect of smaller, unmonitored expenditures that break the budget. That five-dollar daily cup of coffee, those meals you eat out, those magazine subscriptions or TV services that aren't vital—they all add up. There's a big difference between essentials, such as food, and wants, such as premium cable! Review your monthly expenses and eliminate any that aren't necessary.

Pay with Cash

Using cash heightens awareness of what you are spending. For example, Las Vegas casinos use poker chips instead of cash so that people forget they're betting with real money. If you pay with cash, when it's gone, it's gone. You can't spend money that's no longer in your wallet!

Typically, I allow myself a certain amount of cash every month for incidental spending. It's become a sort of game to see if I can still get by on the amount of cash I used to years ago. Guess what? I can and I do! I learned a lot about this by studying Dave Ramsey's envelope system: Let's say you've budgeted $500 a month for groceries. When you get paid, you put that amount into an envelope. No money comes out of that envelope except to buy groceries. If you go to the store and you leave the envelope at home, you turn around and go back for it. In the store, if you spend more than you have in the envelope, you take some groceries out of your cart. If there's no money left in the envelope, you raid your cupboards and the fridge for leftovers.

It's a very simple, effective system to keep in check items that can bust your budget like groceries, entertainment, gas, or clothing. When the money runs out for each category, you simply don't spend any more until the next month.

Get Your Family on the Same Page

A house divided against itself cannot stand. You must get your family members on the same page economically. This can cause some heated debate and argument, but the key to success is to focus on your common financial goals instead of on areas of contention. Discuss as a team what you all value and what you don't. Work together to define your future goals and dreams and what it'll take to reach them.

It only takes thirty days for a repeated activity to become a habit. Make the decision to go all in for thirty days with your new spending and saving habits and they will become routine. A lot of little changes over a short period of time add up—just think of the progress you'll make over six months or a year! Soon, your new habits will be as simple and automatic as making your morning coffee.

Stability

You are financially stable when your income stream is predictable, you're paying your bills on time, and you're not acquiring additional debt—that is, you're living within your means. To fortify your financial foundation you should:

Establish a Home Budget

A home without a budget is like a car without brakes. What's going to stop you from living beyond your means? How do you harness your emotional impulses to purchase? You must establish a budget—and stick to it. Record the amounts that you typically spend in all major home categories and then establish your baseline expenses. This is the most powerful tool for changing impulse purchases into informed decisions.

Develop a Monthly Savings Habit

You already have payments that are automatically withdrawn from your account each month. You must consider monthly deposits into your savings account as a nonnegotiable payment. We've all heard the expression, "Pay yourself first." With this strategy, you're doing that. Start small and then increase the amount over time. As you prosper, increase the amount you transfer every month.

Develop a Debt-Reduction Plan

It's pretty easy to get into debt, but it's not so easy to get out of it. Owing money—be it a mortgage, credit card bills, student loans, or other—can be extremely stressful. When faced with debt, you can feel overwhelmed, powerless, and out of control. It's important to remember that you didn't get into debt overnight, so you can't expect to get out of it immediately. Debt reduction takes time and requires a plan. A great resource to get you started on debt-reduction tactics and techniques is Dave Ramsey's book *The Total Money Makeover.*

Be Properly Insured

Insurance premiums are among the most difficult to make. Having insurance means shelling out money for premiums at regular intervals with the hope that you and your family will never actually need to file a claim on the policy. But without the safety net of insurance, a serious illness, disability, or your death could mean financial ruin for you and your loved ones. You must have sufficient medical, life, and disability insurance if you want to be financially stable. If you don't know a good agent, get a referral from someone you trust for a financial planner or insurance broker. But don't just buy insurance—develop an insurance plan that protects you and your family for the short, mid, and long term.

Have a Written Will

According to a May 2016 Gallup poll, only 44 percent of Americans have made a written will. This means that many Americans are relinquishing control over how their assets will be distributed after they die, as well as who will become guardians of their minor children.

Part of the problem is that many people feel overwhelmed when they think about estate planning. Isn't it complicated and expensive? Not necessarily. A simple will doesn't have to cost very much and is pretty straightforward. Without it, the laws of the state and the decision of a probate court may determine how your estate is distributed and who will care for your kids. Do you want that?

Once you've reached basic financial stability, it's time to focus your sights on reaching the next level of success. Although you've developed the good habits necessary to go to the next step, now is not the time to put your life on autopilot; it's time to change your thinking even more.

Success

You may think you're living on easy street when your income far exceeds your expenses, your savings account is flush, all consumer debt is paid off—and you now actually have disposable income! However, newly acquired financial gains can make you passive and cause you to take your foot off the gas. To reach real financial success, you need to:

Invest in Yourself

We've already spoken at length about the importance of this. Benjamin Franklin had one dominant investment strategy: "If a man empties his purse into his head, no man can take it away from him. An investment in knowledge always pays the best interest." As Jim Rohn once told me, "If you work harder on yourself than you do on your business, you'll go from making a living to making a fortune." Always keep that in mind.

Put Your Money to Work

Putting all your eggs into one basket is dangerous. Invest in stocks, bonds, and real estate. You don't have to be an expert in investing. Get professional advice and invest in what you know. If you don't understand it, don't buy it! And as the saying goes, "If it seems too good to be true, it probably is."

Develop a Detailed Retirement Plan

According to a recent Harris Interactive Poll, 34 percent of Americans have not saved for retirement and 27 percent have no savings at all. Don't be a statistic. If you haven't already, get a referral for a financial adviser who takes a relational, long-term approach to advising his or her customers and plan for your retirement years.

Significance

Significance is the last stage of your financial journey. For many, this is also the time to think about the bigger picture and leaving a legacy. Up until now it's been about you: how you will become financially stable, how you will make more money, and how you will advance in your career. You've been on the path to finding your purpose and significance as you've advanced through the sequence. But once you've reached the success stage, it's natural to begin to think about impacting others. People achieve significance not only by being faithful to wise habits and committing to personal growth and knowledge, but by sharing their knowledge and serving others. They live on through the legacy of their actions and their dedication to the sequence of success.

Have a Plan

Create a plan to sell your business or develop a succession strategy for your heirs to take over after you retire or pass away.

Review Your Portfolio

Reallocate your investment portfolio from growth investments to those that will provide a steady stream of income so you can maintain your lifestyle without working.

Be Intentional with Your Financial Legacy

Whether you're planning to leave money or assets to children or grandchildren, pay for their college, or make bequests to charitable institutions, think through the implication of what the money or assets will mean to those who receive it and how it can help enrich their lives.

Be Charitable

Giving your time and money is an admirable and fulfilling way to live. Giving to charities, causes, and ministries that inspire you is also a great legacy.

A Cautionary Tale

I once knew an immigrant named Sam who came to this country with very little to his name and started a plumbing business. Blessed with the Emigrant Edge, Sam had a great work ethic and provided exceptional customer care, so his business grew and he became successful very quickly. He did lots of work for me, and in turn I referred him to many people.

One day we went to lunch and he asked me about the secret of my success. I shared with him the sequence of the financial journey from survival to significance. Over the next few years, our paths would often cross and we'd have a chance to catch up. From what I could see, he was doing great. He purchased his first home and within three years it had tripled in value. His gross income doubled and he invested in rental property. When I asked if he was following the sequence in order, he always said yes.

Then I got a phone call in the middle of the night. It was Sam—in a complete state of panic. His son was critically ill with a rare virus—he had symptoms of paralysis and his lungs were shutting down. Sam was distraught. "Brian," he said, "we have no health insurance."

I rushed to the hospital, where I was told that the treatment might require a six-month stay and cost between $250,000 and

$500,000. Sam made too much money to qualify for Medicaid, which would have covered the costs.

Because Sam had made successful investments but bypassed the critical stability piece of the sequence—which includes being adequately insured—he was in huge financial trouble. He was forced to sell his rental property and his family's home. The housing market had nosedived since his initial purchase, and he sold his properties for less than eighty cents on the dollar.

Happily his son survived, but Sam learned a very painful lesson about the importance of following the sequence. Here was a man who had done almost everything right, and yet one missing piece had destroyed everything he had built.

Don't make the same mistake. It can be tempting to miss a step because, as you go from survival to significance, you encounter struggle. But struggle is a consequence of advancing through each stage. If you're not struggling, you're not growing. Do you think the caterpillar finds it easy to become a butterfly? Of course not; its internal systems have to morph and grow before it's ready to emerge from its cocoon. The struggles that you feel at each stage are the growing pains necessary to advance to the next. Embrace them and thrive.

CHAPTER TWENTY-FOUR

How to Remember Where You Came From

CHALLENGE 19: KNOW YOUR FAMILY'S HISTORY

Most of us have a natural interest in our family's past. Where did our people, or as the Celts would say our "clan," originate? What were their circumstances; what sorts of relationships did they have; and how did they live, work, and play? These are all questions that ignite our curiosity and make us want to dig deeper into our family history. Why do we have such an intense interest in our past? I believe it's because we want to have a better understanding of ourselves—our past, whether good or bad, is a key to our present.

In years gone by, genealogy was a pursuit of academics and elites. For example, it was common for people to research their family trees to find out if they were related to royalty and nobility. These days, that's no longer the driving motive or desire. Now people just have a hunger to know where they came from so they can have a sense of place and belonging in the world.

Today in America, genealogy is no longer a niche—it's a broad-based, mainstream activity that's accessible to all. Instead of having to spend hours in a library poring over dusty old microfiche or traveling to far-flung destinations to check census data, we have instant access to genealogical databases online. Hard numbers are difficult to come by, but experts believe that genealogy is now the second most popular hobby in the United States after gardening. Is it any wonder? Genealogy is a very user-friendly pastime and you don't even have to get your hands dirty!

> *Remember where you came from. Appreciate where you are. Focus on where you're going.*
> —NICHOLAS J. NICASTRO

Thanks to online archives, genetic testing kits, and websites devoted solely to history, millions of people can research their roots relatively easily from the comfort of their own living rooms. Today you can achieve more in a few hours of research than you could have over a period of many years in the past. And if you hit a dead end, you can always watch a TV show like *Who Do You Think You Are?* to motivate you to keep searching!

I believe it's very important to research your genealogy. Everyone has a story, and your past is part of your identity. But it's one thing to know your family's roots and it's another to actually do something with this information. What lessons can you learn from your predecessors? Some of them may have made mistakes or taken wrong turns, of course, but what are the strengths that have been passed down to you through the generations? What qualities of grit and determination, once displayed in your forefathers' actions and decisions, are reflected in you now? Someone in your bloodline once had resilience, drive, and ambition, and knowing that can unleash inspiration and drive in you today, both grounding and empowering you.

My wife is African American. Our children are very proud of both their Irish and their African ancestry. They know that someone in their bloodline was a slave who came to America not of his or her own free will, but on a slave ship. They know that their great-grandfather was a sharecropper. This knowledge is sobering, but it is also powerful. They're aware they have a responsibility to strive to fulfill the dreams and hopes for a better life that their predecessors sacrificed so much for. Ultimately, we can all pay homage to those in our family tree by doing our best to live up to and fulfill our own potential. What better way to honor those who went before us?

CHALLENGE 20: KNOW YOUR OWN HISTORY

Do you ever find yourself stopping, looking around, and wondering how time passes so quickly? Often this sensation can happen on a special occasion, such as your birthday or New Year's Eve. At different milestones we pause, take stock of what's happened in our life, and wonder where the time has gone. If you have kids, this feeling can be magnified times one million! It can often feel as if one minute they're newborns and the next they're all grown-up with children of their own. When you look back over your shoulder, so to speak, time disappears in the blink of an eye.

I sometimes wish I could freeze time so that I could experience every second of my kids' childhoods all over again, and soak up every precious moment once more, but, of course, that's not possible. Whether we like it or not, time keeps ticking forward, second by second, minute by minute, taking us further and further away from remembrances of the past.

When it comes to our own path toward personal growth and self-discovery, it's important to stop and analyze our journey. How did we get to where we are today? What are the choices we've made that have led us to where we are now? What would we change moving forward? What would we do exactly the same? Remember that movie *Sliding Doors*? In the film, a young woman accidentally misses her train and, because of that one small thing, the trajectory of her life completely changes. We all make a million small decisions every day—each one affects the direction our life takes minute by minute.

There is a pattern to many aspects of the way we live and we repeat patterns in much of what we do—personal behaviors, dynamics in relationships, or financial decisions. If a pattern is destructive— say, becoming involved in harmful relationships or wasting money— it can be difficult to break, especially if we're unaware of it in the first place. Recognizing our patterns can be very useful for analyzing our behavior, but only if we notice them!

In an effort to analyze and record my own patterns, I have kept journals all of my life. I write and reflect on what I did, what I thought, and how I felt at any point in time. Doing so has undoubtedly helped me track my life and thus make sense of my own history.

Key Benefits to Keeping a Journal

Following are some tangible benefits to journaling. *By keeping your own journal, you will:*

Know Yourself Better

How often do we stop to consider how well we really know ourselves? Why do we act the way we do or make the choices we make? What drives us? Inspires us? Motivates us?

Journaling allows you to get to know your inner thoughts and decode the mystery of why you think, feel, and act the way you do. By journaling, you can "find yourself," build a relationship with your inner psyche, and discover what brings you joy and satisfaction. Think of journaling as a one-on-one therapy session for free—it can be a phenomenal source of self-help at your fingertips!

Become More Productive and Powerful

It's easy to forget that an expert in anything was once a beginner too. By tracking your thoughts and activities, you will not only help yourself to manifest your goals, you'll measure your success. There's no better motivation than to look back and see how far you've come—when your progress is laid out in black ink on a page, there's no denying what you've accomplished!

Tap into Your Creative Mind

Did you ever just sit and doodle? Many of us used to do this when we were kids, but as we grew up we lost the habit. Sitting and doodling—or jotting thoughts in a notebook—is a great way to nudge your creativity back into action. Creativity is intelligence having fun, and we all need fun in our lives.

Problem-Solve More Effectively

Sometimes you just can't see the forest for the trees. When you're searching for a solution to a niggling problem, it helps to write your thoughts down. Seeing your thoughts laid out can illuminate the issue better and help you think of solutions you might otherwise have discounted or overlooked. The classic list of pros and cons is proof of this.

Reduce Stress

Stress is a killer, so if there's a simple way to reduce it, then we should grasp it with both hands, right? I believe that journaling is one great way to reduce stress in your life. The act of writing a troubling issue down on paper takes it out of your mind and onto the page. Doing this regularly helps to release the weight of your burdens and ease the stress and strain they cause. The even better news is that as a result of a decrease in stress, conflict with others can reduce and relationships can improve.

Increase Gratitude

According to research, gratitude is one of the most powerful personal resources we have at our fingertips. One of its key benefits is that it helps people feel more connected to each other and more empathetic.

Gratitude is also associated with increased energy and optimism, and it is believed that personal and interpersonal benefits occur at both a psychological and neurobiological level.

Journaling is a great way to turbo-boost the gratitude you experience. Start by writing down a couple of things you are grateful for every day. It can be anything from the hot cup of coffee you had for breakfast to finding a parking space. If you think about it, even when life is difficult, we all experience small daily blessings that we can be thankful for. If you write these down and then read them over, your viewpoint and perspective change—you realize you have a lot to be grateful for and you carry that heartfelt spirit of gratitude into your life and your encounters with others. You become a vessel for gratitude.

In my life, my journals have been more valuable than any checking account. Having a place to reflect on my thoughts, feelings, and actions has given me a very clear picture of myself and my life over time. When you read over an old journal, you get great perspective on how far you have come. You realize that worries that were once overwhelming now seem insignificant; issues you might have struggled with in the past have now been resolved; and problems that you thought would sink you have been overcome. Likewise, you can identify things you still need to work on and improve.

Data is considered to be one of the most valuable resources in the world. Every journey you take and every transaction you make is logged somewhere. Countless companies are gathering data on you right now through your online searches, purchases, and social interactions to better analyze your preferences and choices. If multibillion-dollar corporations recognize the value of data, so should you! Journaling is the ultimate data-gathering exercise and it will unearth a treasure trove of information that will help you.

How to Keep a Journal

Guess what? There's no great secret to keeping a journal! All you need is paper and a pen, or a Word document and a keyboard, if you prefer. *Here are a few tips to get you started:*

Keep It Simple

Many people feel intimidated by the prospect of writing a journal, but it doesn't have to be beautifully written prose and you don't have to produce *War and Peace*. Some days you'll feel like writing a couple of lines, other days you'll fill a page or more. There are no rules. To begin, try documenting the highlights of your day. Where did you go? What did you do? Then think about deeper questions. What did you learn from others? What did you learn about yourself? By the way, don't feel pressure to have perfect spelling or punctuation as you write—perfection is not a requirement.

Keep It Private

This journal is for your eyes only. No one else gets to read it, so feel free to pour out your innermost thoughts. When you have the complete freedom to write whatever comes to mind, it's amazing what can and will end up on the page. Some days your entry will detail simple facts, like what time you got up and where you ate. Other days you'll dig deeper. Over time, all this information paints a picture of who you are, what you stand for, and what you really care about. So let the words flow in whatever random order they want to. Don't worry about how they sound or look on the page—there's no judgment because no one else will ever see it. You don't have to censor or edit yourself—just write what's at the top of your mind.

Make It a Habit

Make a routine of writing. Choose a time that's easiest for you—preferably not when there are a million and one other things screaming for your attention. I like to write either at the beginning or the end of the day. It takes time for a habit to form, so cut yourself some slack if you get off track—if you miss a day, just start again. But *do* start again—don't just give up. If you want to change, you have to make changes!

> *The greatest use of a life is to spend it on something that will outlast it.*
> —WILLIAM JAMES

CHALLENGE 21: PASS IT ON

Legacy videos—keepsake videos in which you document your life for your family—are becoming increasingly popular. If you were to make a legacy video today, what would you say? What would you choose to commemorate and communicate? What would you prefer to leave out? What lessons have you learned? What would you like to pass on?

None of us are here forever. That can be a disquieting thought, but it can also be a galvanizing force! When we're aware of our own mortality, we become more aware of the choices we make and the courses we take. It's good to pay attention to our journey through life. As Socrates famously said, "The unexamined life is not worth living."

Our ultimate significance is not in how smart, rich, or powerful we are, but in how much we serve and give back to others. The more you grow, the more you are able to give.

As I've already said, I'm not a self-made millionaire. There's nothing self-made about me. If I were to make a list of all the people who contributed to my good life, it would take more than all the pages you've read. Authors, mentors, trainers, speakers, friends, family, confidants, and consultants. They've all passed on their wisdom and insight to me, directly and indirectly.

Perhaps the best example of this in my life would be my grandfather. When Granddad would ask me and my brothers his famous question, "Can you put your name to that?" about work we had done, he wasn't asking "Could we get away with this?" or "Did the customer complain?" It was a question about standards. Did it meet the expectations we had for ourselves? If not, then it had to be done over.

My grandfather and my father worked by these principles their whole lives without wavering. Not only did they pass them on to me as a young boy, but I've passed them on to the hundreds of employees at Buffini & Company. The core value of the company is "Excellence is our minimum standard." I have also made sure to pass these principles on to my own children. Although they were born in America, each of them possesses the Emigrant Edge. They are all hard workers and high achievers who "put their names" to everything they do.

"Can you put your name to that?" was a principle that was passed on to me and that I have passed on to others. The seven Emigrant Edge traits are also principles. And principles don't change—tactics do. Principles don't go out of style—fashion does. For example, one of the Ten Commandments is "Thou shalt not kill." It was good advice thousands of years ago and it still holds true today.

When you learn the principles of the Emigrant Edge and employ them in your life, you will change for the better. And then your ultimate responsibility is to pass on what you've done and learned not only to your loved ones, but to other growth seekers you come across on your journey. Embrace the concepts of the Emigrant Edge, apply them to your life, and teach those you know and meet the same principles. Doing this will create a worthwhile and memorable legacy.

In Conclusion

Unleash the Emigrant Edge in Your Life

A nyone with a goal is an emigrant. If you want to move permanently from one place in your life to a better place, you're an emigrant. If you have a goal to improve your health, relationships, career, spiritual life, or financial status, you're an emigrant. We are ALL emigrants.

I wrote this book to both encourage and challenge you. I want to encourage you that it's possible to adopt the Emigrant Edge, no matter where you were born. I also want to challenge you to understand that people come to this country without knowing the language, understanding the culture, or having any resources and they become phenomenally successful. In your backyard!

If they can do it, with all the disadvantages they face, you can certainly do it with all the incredible opportunities and resources you already have at your fingertips. Remember: Their disadvantages are your advantages, and all of their advantages are things you can learn. The beauty of the Emigrant Edge is that it doesn't matter where you were born or where you're going, you can use it to help you flourish.

Unleash the seven traits of the Emigrant Edge in your life and you will experience great success. You must have a voracious openness to learn. You should adopt a do-whatever-it-takes mind-set. You have to be willing to outwork others. You need to embrace a heartfelt spirit of gratitude. You should approach life like a farmer and have a boldness to invest. You must learn to delay gratification for the ultimate attainment of your goals. Finally, you have to remember where you came from and stay grounded. Apply these seven traits in your life and you'll be well on your way to phenomenal success.

You already have everything you need. The Emigrant Edge is in your DNA. Someone in your family history once paid a price to travel across countries, oceans, or mountains so that their children and their children's children would have a better life. Think about it—what would your forefathers do with your set of circumstances? What would they do with the resources and relationships you have? What would they think of your problems compared to the difficulties they faced? They paid a price for you to have the opportunities you have today. Now it's time for you to fulfill that promise.

My challenge to all of you who read this book is that you embrace the Emigrant Edge and go on to experience success and growth in the areas of life that you desire. Then I hope that you pass on this Emigrant Edge mind-set to your loved ones—family, friends, and those you have influence over. I'm the son of a house painter who lives an incredible life today because of the Emigrant Edge. I know if I can do it, you can do it. And if you can do it, so can they.

IN CONCLUSION

As well as to encourage and challenge you, I also wrote this book as a way of saying thank you to the country that made me. I came here with ninety-two dollars in my wallet. I experienced some trials and tribulations here, but I was able to build a very successful life. In this country, I found a passionate and renewed faith in God. I found the love of my life in my wife, Beverly; I've had the privilege of raising six fabulous kids; and I've been able to give my parents a very happy retirement back in Ireland. I've built a business that has employed more than one thousand people, and I've had a chance to serve millions. I've been fortunate enough to spend the last twenty years of my life sharing my principles and practices of success with people. I've traveled to more than 400 cities in this great country, and everywhere I've been, people have embraced my ideas and teachings. It wasn't simple to make it here, but I know it was easier compared to everywhere else.

I'm a proud Irish man and I like to tell my kids I bleed green. However, after almost seventeen years living in my adopted country, on February 19, 2002, I became an American by choice. I did so out of a deep sense of gratitude for what America had done for me. This country accepted me as one of its own. I was a stranger in a strange land, but people gave me a chance. They didn't care where I came from or how I talked. If I served them well, they were willing to work with me, and when I exceeded their expectations, they told their friends.

I remember the swearing-in ceremony like it was yesterday. I was surrounded by more than forty different nationalities, many of whom were in American military uniforms. We all sat waiting for the ceremony to begin. The judge who was supposed to preside over the event was late. Eventually he rushed in, making some excuse about traffic. I remember thinking that wasn't too respectful, considering the gravitas of the occasion. Then he said he hadn't prepared anything to say. Again, I was a little annoyed by this—wasn't he taking this seriously?

But then the judge began to speak. He told the story of a woman who was well educated, had a good job teaching in her homeland, and was well paid for it. However, because of government and social upheaval, she, like many others, was pushed out of her job. She ended up having to work for very little money, sewing clothing to support herself and her two young sons.

Eventually, she saved up enough to send her two boys to America, where they had an aunt and uncle and where she knew they would have the opportunity for a better life. One son finished college, attended medical school, and became a doctor. Her other son went to law school and became an attorney. Eventually he was appointed as a judge.

And then the judge said, "I am that son. I have experienced what all of you have come to experience—the opportunity for a better life. You are not guaranteed happiness, but you are guaranteed the right to pursue happiness. If you work hard, you can make a difference for you and your children."

He went on, "My mother told me to do three things when she sent me to America: First, dream big. Second, work hard. Third, do something to serve others. As new American citizens, I now charge you to do the same thing."

Those three things have stayed in my mind ever since, and I hope as I write this that I have fulfilled the charge I was given that day. Not only have I dreamed big, but dreams have come true that I never thought would happen. I have worked hard and will continue to do so, and I hope my fellow American citizens feel that, as an emigrant, I did something worthwhile to serve them.

Now that you've reached the end of this book, my hope is that you'll feel like *you* just got your brand-new citizenship. I hope something will awaken in you that has always been there—an Emigrant Edge that may have been dormant but will now come alive. I hope you are looking at your opportunities with a fresh perspective and that you have the same hope and anticipation in your heart as newcomers to this land do. The Emigrant Edge that I developed here continues to be the fuel to help me achieve my goals and dreams. Now it's your turn. I want you to take advantage of the opportunities that are in front of you and unleash the principles of the Emigrant Edge to build your own American Dream.

It's a good life!

Brian Buffini

Acknowledgments

A few special thanks:

To Niamh Greene, thank you for your steadfast efforts in help-ing to produce this book. You are a talented wordsmith, a great synergy partner, and your Kilkenny charm helped preserve what I wanted to say and how I wanted to say it.

Thanks to Lisa Stillwell and Philis Boultinghouse for your keen editorial skills. You are both truly gifted at your craft.

To David Lally, who traveled to several continents with me to help make this book a reality.

To Bill Hampton, Dermot Buffini, Terri King, Joan Buffini, and Jonathan Merkh for your guidance and honest feedback.

ACKNOWLEDGMENTS

To Beverly and the A-Team, if I had known I would have been with you, I would have emigrated sooner.

Special thanks to all the clients of Buffini & Company, who have impacted and improved the lives of millions of people.